LISTEN TO THE GOSPELS

LISTEN TO THE GOSPELS

by

Richard Ferguson

The Memoir Club

First published in 2011 by
The Memoir Club
Arya House
Langley Park
Durham
DH7 9XE
Tel: 0191 373 5660
Email: memoirclub@msn.com

ISBN: 978-1-84104-534-4

Printed by Xpresslitho, Washington, Tyne & Wear

To Liz, my wife, So much more than just my 'Better Half.'

Contents

List of Illustrations

Acknowledgements

No one can say with absolute certainty just what influences have contributed to writing a book such as this. I am not a scholar – but have been immensely grateful to many a scholar whose writings have given me food for thought and knowledge to inform. But I write, more as pastor and teacher since I have been a parish priest for more than forty years, and even in retirement am driven by the same passion for people and Christ and the Gospel.

It has been my great good fortune to serve under two men of great stature, and I cannot but feel that their influence on me has a very great deal to do with what follows. The first was Canon Frank Wright, whose curate I was when I began my ministry. Everything I know about the pastoral ministry and serving as a priest I owe to him – his wisdom and care for the people he served; he was a great preacher, and worship in his hands was always uplifting. His tireless attention to the needs, both of the Church as a community and to individuals, was remarkable. His influence lives on, and I am immensely grateful to Jane (Carlin), Simon and Roger Wright who have between them written the Foreword for this book. What a talented family!

I also had the privilege to be, for fifteen short months, Domestic Chaplain to Ian Ramsey, Bishop of Durham. He was a man of large intellect, yet he was utterly at home in the company of ordinary people. He listened with great intensity, no matter who you were, and took infinite pains with whatever was presented to him. I remember still one of his Confirmation sermons; it took great themes, but expressed them in words that even the youngest teenager could understand and respond to. He wrote, he taught, he challenged those around him to higher things. Above all, he inspired; no Bishop could do more. His memory is still an inspiration.

In the writing of this book, Dr Jennifer Soutter has been my editor. In fact, she has been a great deal more, and I am immensely grateful for her skill, her patience and her expertise. I would also like to thank Canon Richard Bryant who read the text and offered a host of helpful suggestions.

Finally I would like to thank my publishers, The Memoir Club, for daring to take on an unknown writer, and steering me through a world that seemed so daunting when I began.

Richard Ferguson 2011

The text used throughout is *The Revised English Bible*[1]

---

[1] Oxford University Press and Cambridge University Press, 1989.

Foreword

It was with enormous pleasure that we read Richard Ferguson's acknowledgements in writing this book. Richard was one of our father's curates at the Parish Church of St Matthew's, Stretford in the Manchester diocese in the 1960s. His description of what he learned from him is thoughtful and generous. Our father held him in high regard and would no doubt be thrilled by the publication of this book - not least for its plain speaking challenge, encouraging us to look at the Gospels in a fresh light as individual books, not four re-workings of the same story. No doubt he would also endorse the strong sense of this book being centred on the idea of pastoral work for the church - if the people of God are assisted in their interpretation of the gospels, then their mission will be more meaningful. This book will certainly help them on their journey of understanding.

Jane Carlin, Simon and Roger Wright

Introduction

Bursting into Print . . .

I am not one of those people who feel the need to burst into print whenever they see something wrong. I have occasionally written to the papers – but only very occasionally – so this is not a knee-jerk reaction to something I have noticed, and want to get off my chest. Over a matter of years I have been getting increasingly alarmed at what I see, but frequently dismissed it as an old man thinking things were better 'in the old days.' I am, after all, retired. I have served forty years in the parish ministry of the Church of England, working in parishes as far apart as Slough and North Shields, Oldham and Kirkwhelpington (Northumberland). Retirement has been busy – as it often is for retired parish priests. I have preached more than 250 times in those six years and been grateful for the opportunity to make a contribution to the life of the Church as far as I can.

In one sense, retirement has been a blessing. I have had a forty-year itch which has been niggling me; I've scratched it every now and then, and produced a number of documents which have been invaluable in parish life. The Gospel of Mark was usually the focus of attention. Somehow it had caught my imagination when at university, and during my first curacy I set about writing things down. It took years to complete – a layman's commentary, I grandly called it, on the Gospel according to St Mark. Its title may well have been the best thing about it – *Victory through Suffering* – but it served well for confirmation classes and other study groups, and for a while the itch was silenced. By the time I had a sabbatical in Oxford in 1989 all the copies were gone, and it was more than time to revisit the subject and write something else that I could use in the parish setting. I went to lectures and did some supervised writing. What astonished me was how little things had seemed to have changed since I was last in college. My books were a generation old, but the same subjects seemed to be coming up, and were tackled in much the same way as I remembered. This left me feeling uneasy – surely things had changed – but sabbaticals do not last for ever, and soon enough the demands of parish life, and then a change of parish swamped any ideas of further scratching the itch which still had not gone away.

It was when I joined a group studying St Mark's Gospel in the Greek that the itch became serious again. By then we were living in Northumberland, nearly twenty miles from Newcastle where the group met, and the combination of distance as well as parochial and deanery duties meant that my attendances were intermittent (and that is being kind!). However, the failure to see it through properly produced a penance: when Lent was over, I told myself, I would set to and make my own translation of Mark's Gospel. It took nine months – and a further nine months to learn it. I had heard the Gospel recited some years before and been both stimulated and appalled in almost equal measure: I could not get on with the long white robe the speaker wore, or the scenery he had employed to give what he hoped would be a feeling of Palestine in Jesus' time. I was equally unimpressed with the translation (I cannot now remember which one); it was stilted, I thought, and did not communicate to me anything of the power and the directness which is a characteristic of this Gospel. Could I do any better?

I trust the answer has been 'yes,' and since those days I have recited St Mark's Gospel probably fifty times. Occasionally, the Gospel was unintentionally rewritten (*mea ulpa!*), since I am not renowned for a particularly good memory, but the reaction of people hearing this man reciting the Gospel in this way (I call it 'recital'; surely there must be a better word?) was astonishing. In particular, the stunning silence which on almost every occasion followed the closing words of the Gospel sent me back to examine the whole experience and what it meant. What people said was, 'I've never heard the Gospel spoken in one go. It's amazing – powerful – thought-provoking – mind-blowing!' I could not agree more, but the problem is that the Gospel is never presented in this way. Usually, we hear one episode, just a few verses are plucked out of the air and put in the context of a service, when there is so much going on around it. Even the (relatively) new lectionary expects us to be able to remember what we heard from week to week! In fact, the way the lectionary treats St Mark's Gospel is less than helpful, not least when it comes to the feeding of the five thousand in chapter 6. By substituting John's account of the event along with the very Johannine arguments which follow, the flow of the Gospel is destroyed.

The reasoning that must have gone into such a considered action is very telling. It treats the Gospels as if they were all the same, and assumes that the account of an event in one Gospel can be treated in the same way as the account of the same event in another Gospel. John's account of the feeding of the five thousand and the walking on the water is different both in context and the details of the story, not to mention the way it is used in each Gospel.

What may also be that behind the decision to use texts in this way is the assumption that each Gospel is written from the same point of view – to tell the Jesus story and to inform its readers (or hearers) of the events of his life. This is an enormous assumption, but, far more importantly, it forces the Gospels into a strait-jacket in which none of them fit comfortably.

I need hardly say that the itch was becoming more serious rather than less, and in 2007 I realised that I would have to go back to the computer and put my developing thoughts into print. This happened, but with a difference. *Rocks and Breakers* did three things: it presented in print for others to use the translation I had made a few years before, and with it light comments to help readers get into the text. It was not a commentary in any sense of the word; its purpose was to open the Gospel to people who had no knowledge of it whatever (and no habit of Bible-reading either) so that the Gospel itself would be able to speak more easily to readers in the twenty-first century. It was a friend of mine who read through the draft version of 'Rocks and Breakers' and suggested that I should include not only the written text but also the text spoken on CDs. It made sense. If the case I was making was that this Gospel was an oral work originally, the book should enable people to hear it.

The result was a 'do-it-yourself' job – I did not think a publisher would look at a book which was anything but academic, and which included CDs. I persuaded a local printer to produce the book, and made a recording of the text which was put on two CDs. I find that people make great use of the recording, and listen to it in extraordinary circumstances (not least travelling to work!).

But itches are very persistent, and although I have been giving 'recitals' and selling copies of 'Rocks and Breakers' on request, the print was hardly dry before I realised that at some point a fuller account of my approach would have to be given. I had, in a few short paragraphs, outlined an approach to the differences in the Gospels (one of the causes of puzzlement and confusion about the Gospels which is very widespread) without going into it in great detail, and certainly not backing up my approach with any real body of evidence or reasoning. That was not the purpose of the book.

Now the matter has become urgent. In Lent 2010 a good number of people in the north-east of England had taken part in a reading of St Luke's Gospel. On two occasions it was our turn to host such a group, and obviously I was part of the group on those occasions, although as a rule clergy in such groups tend to take over and defeat the whole purpose of the group. I kept as quiet as I could, but beneath the surface discussion I heard confusion, uncertainty as to how to read it, what to make of the differences between the

Gospels, and a host of other symptoms which suggested that a lifetime of churchgoing had left these people (nice, intelligent, faithful people who had heard all the passages a hundred times before) quite unable to sit down and make sense of the text in front of them.

That is what sets the agenda for this book. Whatever the reason may be, the Gospels are not simple reading. People of this generation cannot, as their forebears did, simply pick up the Bible and read what is written and accept it as 'gospel.' We have become more complicated, and such is the culture of questioning, if not doubting, everything we are told that even the most straightforward of accounts is examined and tested in a way that would have been unthinkable a hundred years ago. Many people come to the New Testament with questions in their mind. The Bible no longer has that unquestioned authority it once had, and people want to know more and to be certain of what they are being told. It is also true that in a culture where Bible-reading is much less common, many more people are coming to texts with which they are not familiar, and bringing to those texts an approach which belongs more to the secular world of the twenty-first century than the worshipping community of past generations.

In many ways the key word to this study is context. We need to be aware of how our context has changed in recent years, because it is context which in many ways shapes our approach to the Gospels. People who are searching need to know about Jesus; they need information as well as encountering his person through the pages of the New Testament. Those who have committed themselves to follow Jesus are looking for guidance, teaching, inspiration to stimulate faith, social engagement and aid personal devotion. This is part of the context which is an essential aspect of the way we use the texts handed down to us.

At the same time, everything in life has a context, even the Gospels, and it will also be their context which helps us to see them in focus and understand what they are telling us. But this is where we run into a brick wall. Whatever context each Gospel originally had is lost, not least because they have been given an entirely new context – the New Testament. They did not begin their life as Holy Scripture, and it was the Church which invested in them the great authority they have had since the second century. We might say, they have two contexts: the one which the Church gave them as presenting a true and faithful picture of Jesus, between them telling us all we need to know to believe truly in Jesus Christ; the other context is the situation, probably within the life of the young, growing and changing Church, which shaped the way each came into being and the content each was given.

This study sets out to look for the second of these two contexts in the hope (and belief) that it will make the reading of the Gospels more fulfilling, and that it will help us to understand the differences which so confuse even those who have considerable knowledge already, accumulated over years of hearing the scriptures read in Church and in their own private study.

I am bound to say that as a preacher for forty-five years and more I may not have helped those in my pastoral care very much. The temptation of every preacher is to draw in whatever material will help the theme of the sermon along. Too often sermons begin with a set of words – probably taken from the readings of the day – without exploring or taking much account of the setting in which they are found in the Bible. When other words from elsewhere seem to add to what is being spoken about, how often they are 'borrowed,' also without reference to where they come from, let alone what they mean in that setting. Now that I am in the pew rather more frequently, I realise how often this happens, and how our lay people are not helped to approach the texts we have been given when preachers treat them in this way. We all need a framework to help us in our approach to the passages we are reading, not least an understanding of the context, which will help us see the deeper references and insights which so often context provides.

In this study, we shall be concentrating on the Gospels themselves. Since my student days I have spent so much time reading what others have said about the Gospels. I believe this is a distraction; sometimes we have been led away from the Gospels, and so have not picked up the hints and the clues which each of them gives us. It is the Gospels themselves which will tell us what kind of a work each is, the circumstances which prompted its creation, and what was in mind as the creative process worked itself out.

This is not to take away for one moment from the unique importance of the four canonical Gospels of the New Testament. They are the most important books that we have. They talk in human terms about the most fundamental things in life: they speak of God; they speak of the purpose of life; they give us the possibility of a personal relationship with the One through whom life is transformed and eternal life is possible. If for no other reason than that the Gospels provide us with the unique experience of resurrection, these are the books which every mortal needs to read and study and value.

This book is written to enable people to open the Gospels with confidence, and find their lives enriched and changed by what they read there. It is time for the journey to begin.

As my text I have used *The Revised English Bible*, Oxford University Press and Cambridge University Press, 1989.

CHAPTER ONE

Gospels – The Beginnings

To begin at the beginning seems only sensible. To begin a study of the Gospels by looking at the opening words of each Gospel is rather more unusual. But there is a point: the opening words of any act of communication are important, whether it is a book or a speech, an essay or a sermon. Where the author chooses to start gives the answer to a whole plethora of questions, most of which are never actually put into words, but they are important nevertheless: what kind of work is this? With whom am I communicating? What do I want them to take from it? How will they receive it? By the time the first words take shape these and many other questions have been answered.

When we read or hear the words, 'Once upon a time,' we know we are in fairy-tale country, and can expect a story of make-believe, and probably an ending which speaks of the main characters in the story living 'happily ever after.' Other kinds of literature may not quite have the same give-away opening, but their features are just as distinctive. A novel will begin in a different way from an essay or a thesis; storytelling is very different from setting out a detailed academic proposition, and painstakingly developing the arguments which bring it to its proper conclusion. A speech is very different from either of these ways of communicating. The context in which a speech is to be delivered and the nature of the audience are essential factors in determining the starting point, and the way the subject is approached. Beginnings, however unconsciously, spell out to the reader (or listener) the nature of what lies ahead.

No such considerations have usually been applied to the four Gospels of the New Testament. They come to us as 'Gospels,' and as such are seemingly unique in the literature of their day. Others imitated them, but there was no particular kind of literature in existence which set out a pattern for the Gospel-writers to follow. That, in itself, is remarkable, and speaks of the power and the originality of the experience and the faith which gave rise to them. All of them speak of Jesus of Nazareth, his life and teaching, his death and resurrection. As to how they came into being and when, there is no definitive answer – though much speculation. By the middle of the second century, however, these four Gospels were in circulation throughout most parts of the Church, and by then had been accorded a place of pre-eminence in the life of the Church. They were taken together, and seen together as containing all a person needed to know and believe about Jesus of Nazareth to be able live the Christian faith. In some parts of the Church, they circulated without the ascription with which we are familiar ('The Gospel according to Matthew/Mark/Luke/John'), but soon enough this title became fixed. It may well be that giving them such a title was thought to invest them with even further authority (Matthew and John are the names of Apostles; Mark was thought to have been a close follower of Peter – Papias, c AD 135 – and Luke was doctor to and travelling companion of Paul, the great Apostle to the Gentiles). But this was a notion others borrowed as well, as we see from 'The Gospel of Peter,' 'The Gospel of Barnabas,' even 'The Gospel of Judas,' which all appeared in the next hundred years. Most of these gospels were written to put forward a particular view of Jesus and the Christian life which was at odds with the orthodox teaching the Church had developed – signs of the growing pains of the Church.

The four canonical Gospels had become utterly central to the life of the Church in a way that those who brought them into being cannot have envisaged. Whether their creators intended it or not, they became the central scriptures of the Christian Church, and were only joined by the other books which now make up the New Testament decades later. It was inevitable that the Church would over time set out its own sacred writings. The Jews had done the same at Jamnia in AD 95, and fixed the shape of their scriptures (the Old Testament, as Christians know it), although many of the books involved had been in existence for hundreds of years. It was essential for the Christian community to have its own scriptures, both to set out its faith and to differentiate the Christian faith from that of the Jews.

If we find it odd that there are four Gospels, we are not the first. In the middle of the second century, Tatian compiled the 'Diatessaron.' It was an attempt to make one single account of Jesus' life and work, using the material from all four of the Gospels. For a while it prospered, and was widely used in some parts of the Church, but by about the fifth century it had fallen out of favour, and the four Gospels prevailed. But the very fact that it was attempted suggests that having four different accounts of Jesus' life and teaching, death and resurrection grated then, just as many people today find the differences between the Gospels puzzling and confusing. It seems odd to have four accounts of a single life.

There have, of course, been attempts to help us live more comfortably with what we have received. Over the last 100 years an inordinate amount of time and effort has been expended on exploring the relationship between the first three Gospels, suggesting how they might have come about. It was talked about as the 'synoptic problem.' Scholars over the years have noted a host of similarities between the first three Gospels – the general order of events, much material in common and an approach to telling the story of Jesus which was so similar that many a reader found it easy to confuse one account with another. Many thought that Mark wrote his Gospel first, and that Matthew and Luke used Mark's Gospel as a basis for their own, adding their own material to fill out Mark's rather shorter account. While this was the most widely accepted solution, opinion was by no means unanimous; in any case, scholars were remarkably vague about what they meant by 'used' or 'copied.' In the end, even this approach has run into the ground, and we are left with a feeling that there is 'something there,' but with no real certainty what the relationship really was.

It is the merit of starting with the opening words of each Gospel that much of this great body of material is left on one side, and we are free to lay our own foundations for a study which is both fresh and focussed. Some ground rules will be important. Each of the Gospels will be considered as a work in its own right. They come to us as 'Gospels,' but it is more important than anything else to listen to what each Gospel has to say about itself. We must not assume that simply because they came to us as a group they belong together; it was the Church which brought them together to meet its own needs – and that happened generations after they each came into being. That must seem a strange way to talk about the writing of the Gospels. It seems so obvious that what has come down to us in document form was written by someone at some time – but that is part of the problem we have inherited: we have labelled the Gospels, called them holy writ and given them an authority that is utterly unique, and attached to them a name (Matthew, Mark, Luke, John) which suggests that they were written by someone who might be able to be identified – and along with the Gospels we have inherited centuries of comment that have reinforced these descriptions. But were all the Gospels written documents when they were created? Have we concentrated far too much on the identity of writers, rather than asking what kind of work each is? Do they all have the same purpose, the same audience in mind?

The purpose of this study is to listen to what the Gospels have to say about themselves. Each will give its own indications about its origin and purpose; each will give us clues as to whom each Gospel was addressed. Each will make it clear by its use of language and content whether it was written or spoken, when it was initially conceived. That is what makes this study so exciting. As we allow the Gospels to speak to us, it may well be that we shall be shown unexpected facets of each; it is very much hoped that what emerges will help us to understand the differences which now puzzle us. It may even help us to use the Gospels more effectively; not only in our own discipleship, but also in the way we commend the Christian Way to others.

We will take the Gospels in the order in which they appear in the New Testament. That is not to imply that one Gospel came before the others – not necessarily in the order of appearance; it is simply how we have received them.

MATTHEW'S GOSPEL

St Matthew begins his Gospel: *The genealogy of Jesus Christ, son of David, son of Abraham.'* (Matthew 1:1)

Matthew is not the first to begin his writing with a genealogy; 1 Chronicles, one of the later books of the Old Testament, also begins in this way. This is Matthew's choice. Very deliberately he is setting out the framework within which his record is to be understood. It is a very Jewish background, and it embraces a great number of Jewish practices and patterns of thought. The genealogy is traced through the male line, following the pattern of the Jewish scriptures as a whole, not just 1 Chronicles.

Matthew calls Jesus *'Christ.'* To a Jew, this title needs no explanation. Few things united the Jews more powerfully than the expectation that one day the promised Messiah would come: he it is who is to bring about all that God had promised to his chosen people. As if to confirm this, Jesus is described as *'son of David, son of Abraham,'* the two great figures from Jewish history to whom God had given his promises. To David, God had promised a king to sit on his throne and rule over the promised kingdom. To Abraham God had promised that all nations would be blessed through his offspring.

In just a few words Matthew gives us a strong indication of what this Gospel is about. It is about Jesus of Nazareth. But it is not to be a biography: Matthew is to tell the story of how this Jesus fulfilled all God's promises to his chosen people, and lived out his calling as God's Messiah. He begins with Jesus' family tree, starting with Abraham, the patriarch; Jesus is a Jew through and through, and so is equipped from the human point of view to fulfil his divine calling.

But there is more to these opening words than just what we have in front of us. Behind these opening words are a number of decisions which Matthew does not put into words. Quite deliberately, he has taken up the method and patterns of the scriptures with which he was familiar. But he is not only copying the Jewish scriptures; he is intentionally writing scripture himself, placing his book firmly in a well-established tradition of great importance. He intends his book to be read as scripture is read, and he believes that what he is recording brings to completion everything of which the Jewish scriptures spoke. His Gospel, then, is not just written in imitation of the scriptures he knew: he believed that his record belongs to those scriptures because it completed the purposes of God to which they bore witness. Perhaps he even thought that his Gospel completed the Jewish scriptures, and that his writings were the final chapter in God's glorious dealings with his people.

As the Gospel unfolds, we shall see Matthew not only referring to the prophets and God's word to his people in the Old Testament. Matthew freely takes up other familiar means of communication: so, before the end of the first chapter, we shall encounter angels and dreams which are to be found in the later books of the Jewish scriptures especially. It is almost as if he is at pains to make sure that his readers are aware that his writing belongs to this tradition, and that he is signalling continuity with them.

With this emphasis on scripture, it goes without saying that this is a written document, and Matthew uses the strengths of the written word to help him. We shall have quotations from scripture; there will be lists (the genealogy is only the first), and Matthew will not be shy to record directions and instructions on living the Christian life in passages of instruction. Only the written word would be able to carry such material, since it primarily seeks to inform and explain; it assumes a relationship with its audience of giving and receiving of information, with the aim of communicating understanding and knowledge.

Who, then, did Matthew have in mind as he wrote? It would be tempting to suggest that Matthew was writing primarily for those who knew and valued the Jewish scriptures. But they are his starting point, not necessarily his intended audience. What is clear is that his whole approach, speaking of God and the fulfilment of his promises in the person of Jesus, is intended for the faith community, in particular those for whom faith in the Jesus he is presenting is paramount. By the time he wrote, a great divide will have opened up between the Jewish and Christian faiths, and while his Gospel speaks of the things the Jews cherish and believe in, only the Christian community will be ready to hear and live by the way of the discipleship he sets out. Matthew's intention has, from the first, been to provide scripture for the Christian community. As such it still speaks to us today.

MARK'S GOSPEL

'The beginning of the gospel of Jesus Christ the Son of God.' (Mark 1:1)

The opening words of St Mark's Gospel could hardly be more direct. There is no question of any literary form being followed. Whether reader or listener, we are being addressed without form or convention wrapping up what Mark is saying. There is no careful laying of foundations: verse 1 is title, contents and introduction all rolled into one! The storyline begins in verse 2.

Mark alone of the four speaks of itself as a 'Gospel.' Whether Gospel should have a capital 'G' – referring to the book as a whole, and giving it a special identity – or whether the author is simply talking about the 'good news' of Jesus which is about to unfold as the account gets underway must remain open for the moment. The first might suggest that there were written accounts of the good news of Jesus already in existence that had acquired the title of 'Gospel,' and what is about to begin is the Gospel according to St Mark. But this gives a rather self-conscious estimate of the work that is beginning, which is at odds with the directness of the opening and the style of the Gospel as a whole. The lack of literary form and the directness of the language suggests that we must at least be open to the possibility that the natural manner for these words to be used is through the spoken word – that the word Gospel refers to the giving of the good news, and that is about to happen as the speaker takes up his task. It is in the nature of things that in the very early days of the Church all 'gospelling' would have been done orally, person to person. What we have in front of us could well be one of the ways Christians developed of telling others of Jesus and inviting them to come to believe in him as well.

It would be natural to expect the good news to be about Jesus – but the text is more direct than that: he is the good news, and the news is that Jesus is both Christ and Son of God. This reading of the opening words is confirmed by the shape of the Gospel as a whole. The two titles Jesus is given in this opening verse appear at critical junctures in the Gospel. We are being prepared for what lies ahead; for the Gospel has two halves, each leading up to a moment of recognition, a moment which for each half is the climax to which the previous chapters have been leading.

But it is the moments of recognition which give us the clue as to what this Gospel is all about. Mark is not just about telling the story of Jesus and giving us an account of all he said and did. This Gospel has a style and a sense of purpose from the very beginning. In very few words a great deal is said, and as the Gospel develops we shall find this same brevity in all that is recorded, We shall also find a strong connectedness between one passage and the next, so that one event leads into, and prepares us for, the next. Where a link is difficult, the authors provide one, so that the audience is continually moved forward as the drama of the Gospel builds. But what is driving this continuity is the determination to bring the audience themselves to moments of recognition; the authors want their audience to be involved more than merely informed, challenged rather than merely interested.

This is a dynamic which belongs more easily with the oral rather than the written. What is also being suggested is that this Gospel is intended to be heard by those who are not yet members of the Church. It is a response to interest and enquiry from outside the faith community, and as such naturally belongs to the 'gospelling' activity of the Church. Of the four Gospels, it would seem that this is the Gospel which most clearly fulfils the title 'Gospel.'

LUKE'S GOSPEL

'To Theophilus: Many writers have undertaken to draw up an account of the events that have taken place among us, following the traditions handed down to us by the original eyewitnesses and servants of the gospel. So I in my turn, as one who has investigated the whole course of these events in detail, have decided to write an orderly narrative for you, your excellency, so as to give you authentic knowledge about the matters of which you have been informed.' (Luke 1:1-4)

The opening passage of Luke's Gospel is long and involved; no one is going to find his attention grabbed and held by the way Luke begins his writing – a very different beginning from St Mark's Gospel. This is very much a written work. Luke begins by carefully laying out the project in front of him: he is aware of other documents, but he seems more than sceptical about their value, and contrasts what he is setting out to do with those other less than satisfactory accounts. The opening itself is very formal, literary in style, and carefully crafted. He certainly seems to be trying to impress.

The contrast between this opening and the first sentences of Matthew's and Mark's Gospel could not be clearer. He can take nothing for granted, and in the respectful way in which he addresses Theophilus he almost seems nervous about the reception he will get. Perhaps that is why Luke takes refuge in such a formal opening. In fact, this kind of formal opening was quite widely used in his day as a way to begin a learned treatise. Anyone acquainted with the world of study would have been familiar with such an opening; Luke wants his account to be taken very seriously.

We are, of course, studying the Gospel ascribed to Luke, but the Acts of the Apostles also addresses Theophilus, and begins with the same formality. So close are the beginning and end points of the two books that is seems probable that Luke is the author of both. By the same token, the events referred to in this opening passage may well also include events now related in the Acts of the Apostles. Luke's two books became separated when the four Gospels were grouped together, with the result that many people studying the Gospel today consider it in isolation, rather than as the first volume of a two-volume project. But the books belong together, and suggest that the scope of the project was not just to pass on accurate information about Jesus of Nazareth, but also to speak with authority about the life and growth of the young Church. After the initial account of the birth of the Church at Pentecost and its very early days in Jerusalem, much of the Acts of the Apostles follows Paul's missions around the eastern end of the Mediterranean, and ultimately his arrival in Rome. What is particularly intriguing is the way the author begins to talk not about 'they' and 'them', but 'we' (Acts 16:10), suggesting that the author himself was taking part in Paul's travels and the dangers that were encountered. It seems more than possible that the writer Luke becomes part of the story, and is able to recount some of the dramatic events, not least the shipwreck (Acts 27 and 28), from his own experience. For the moment, perhaps, we need do no more than note that this opening passage begins a two-volume undertaking which leads the reader from the birth of John the Baptist to the arrival of the Gospel at Rome.

As noted earlier, both his books are addressed to Theophilus. Whether this is a particular individual, or whether it is addressed more generally to an audience in the Roman world is always a matter of debate, especially as Theophilus means 'lover of God.' It is just as possible that his writing was really being addressed more generally to people outside the Church who were thoroughly sceptical about this new upstart religion. The fact that Luke speaks of other accounts suggests that he is looking beyond the immediate matter in hand, and also that the real intention was for his writings to have a much wider audience than just one person, however eminent.

Luke is not writing biography. His intention is to set out a record which is reliable because it has been thoroughly researched, and which can give his audience the kind of information with which they can make a judgement about Jesus and about his followers. There will be biographical details (and Luke gives us many more personal details than any other Gospel), but he is even more anxious to put on record the things that would enable those who have no great knowledge of things Jewish to come to an understanding of Jesus and his significance, not just for the Jewish people, but for people of every race and nationality. This Gospel is addressed to the Gentile world, and sets out a case to which everyone is invited to respond.

JOHN'S GOSPEL

'In the beginning the Word already was. The Word was in God's presence, and what God was, the Word was.' (John 1:1)

The opening of St John's Gospel is one of the most famous first sentences in all literature. What sounds so simple is both profound and complex. The beginning of which it speaks is not of this Gospel, nor even the beginning of the story of Jesus: John speaks on a cosmic scale, and the beginning which is his starting-point takes us back to creation – and before. After three Gospels which speak through the life, death and resurrection of Jesus, this opening sentence is bound to take us by surprise: we have to adjust the way we approach the story of Jesus, and try to understand what we are told against an eternal backdrop, not just the span of a human life. But this is right and proper. The other three Gospels have started with the human, but pointed us beyond the mortal and material to the activity of the eternal God among us. John begins with the eternal, so that we shall never lose sight of the abiding truth of Christ, or get so preoccupied with the physical and human experience of him, that we never arrive at a faith which allows Jesus to be fully God.

John speaks of 'the Word' – and in so doing embraces two very different worlds. The Jews knew and understood about the Word of God. It had been spoken through the prophets; it had been spoken through Moses, through whom God's commands were given. Their history could not be understood without the Word of God at the very heart of their life as the Chosen People. At the same time, the Word also spoke to the world of Greek philosophy. Since the halcyon days of Plato the Word – meaning 'reason' – had held sway and been extremely powerful in shaping the way people came to understand the world and life and truth. But soon we shall learn that through his use of the Word John not only invites both Jew and Greek to bring their understanding to the truth he is setting out; he intends to take them beyond what they already know, and share with them a new understanding of the Word, expressed through the life, death and resurrection of Jesus of Nazareth. His new understanding is: *'So the Word became flesh; he made his home among us, and we saw his glory, such glory as befits the Father's only Son, full of grace and truth.'* (John 1:14)

This opening sentence gives us an indication of John's real intention. This is not straight storytelling, even though the heart of it will be the life, death and resurrection of Jesus. These events are real enough – some of them utterly staggering – but the message John will communicate is going to be on an entirely different level. So brief is this opening that it has all the hallmarks of an oral credo. It is a proclamation of faith. What John is doing is expressing the conviction with which he approaches the task of setting out the eternal truths to be found in the life of Jesus; these are the truths which undergird everything he writes. We need to take this vision with us when the narrative begins; there will be no understanding his Gospel without first having grasped the conviction from which he writes; this he sets out in the first seventeen verses. We are invited to share his conviction so that we can also grasp the good news he is offering us.

But for whom is this astonishing book intended? This is the one Gospel for which the answer to this question is not obvious. He seems to be speaking to the point at which faith and reason meet. It may well be, therefore, that he is aiming to communicate at more than one level – and possibly to more than one kind of audience. It is clear that he expects his audience to be able to respond to his reference to the Word, and to appreciate the significance of this fundamental vision. But this opening reference does not belong to the world of ideas alone: he speaks with the conviction of faith, while giving expression to faith in terms often reserved for reason. What is certainly true is that his writing has proved both challenging and inspirational; it speaks at a depth other Gospels do not attempt to reach, and for that reason alone this Gospel adds a vital dimension to the sacred writings on which the Church draws.

Not quite what they seem

Our first glance at the Gospels suggests that we have four documents that are very different in nature and purpose. The reason why they are placed side by side and given a unique standing in the life of the Church is as much to do with the needs of the Church in the second century as the different situations in the first century from which they arose. They have served the Church well, and remain for all Christians their most important documents, speaking as no other writings do of the Jesus who is Lord and God.

The little we have seen has suggested that at least one of them is fundamentally an oral work, which may well have developed into the shape in which we have it through the whole process of sharing the good news orally – person to person. Another is consciously writing scripture, primarily for use within the Church where teaching about living the Christian life was paramount. Another is part of a two-volume treatise commending the Church and the Christian faith to a hostile and cynical world, while the final document is an extraordinary mixture of polemic and reflection on Jesus, which would have been a powerful witness to the truth of Christ both in the secular world at large, where Greek philosophy had widely shaped the way people thought, and among the Jewish community. What a diverse collection!

What we have been shown, however, indicates the importance of context. Much of the study of the Gospels over the years has concentrated on the individual writers. There has been so much speculation both about their identity and the driving forces which prompted them to put pen to paper. Everything in life has a context, and we have been given the strongest hint, even in these opening verses, that context has been the factor which has shaped each Gospel, and that the changing needs of the growing and expanding Church have been the real guiding factors in each case. Our study, therefore, marks a real change in the way we approach the Gospels and our understanding of what they are communicating to us.

The Gospels are not just different versions of the same thing. Their starting points demonstrate that they came into being in different ways and for different reasons. Their content, when we get to it, will underline how carefully they have been crafted to meet the purpose for which they were created. It must be less than helpful, therefore, to treat them as if they were the same, trying to communicate an identical message. They are not. Their very variety frees us to approach the Gospels from different directions; they speak to us of different aspects of God's great activity in Jesus.

At the same time, we also need to be aware of the context in which we read them and listen to them. It is not just that we approach the Gospels with questions (that would have been unheard of 100 years ago!); we have expectations which the authors of these unique books had not dreamt of. Many people coming to the Gospels for the first time look for historicity (as defined in our own day); they, so close to the living experience of Jesus, saw no need to labour this point; we wonder about miracles; they would ask what more evidence we wanted. The context of our world shapes our reading, just as the context of their day shaped the way they recorded the things which were to them so sacred. We are conscious of the time that has elapsed; for them, time was the immaterial.

As this study unfolds, we will be challenged to look in a new way at things that are familiar (to some) and sacred. In every case, the good news of Jesus was powerful and transforming; it is hoped that the approach this study is suggesting will allow some of that living quality to inform and shape our thinking too.

CHAPTER TWO

Mark – The Spoken Word

It is one of the ironies of history that St Mark's Gospel would not have come to us had it not been written down. It is as a written document that it was ranked with the other great Gospels, and as such has been read and studied ever since. Yet the opening words of the Gospel suggest that its shape and character are those of an oral work, and that it was as an oral work that it was first used by the Church. Since not many people could read in those days, it was inevitable this Gospel would mainly have been spoken, but the suggestion that it is originally an oral work goes somewhat further. The oral and the written have very different strengths and characteristics, and we need to be alert to them as we examine the Gospels and allow them to speak to us.

For centuries, the written word has been our primary means of communication – it has so many advantages, especially since the advent of the computer, which has revolutionised the way we store knowledge and communicate with one another; even the mobile phone is used as much for texting as it is for speaking. What is written down can be checked and referred to again and again; it can carry information, even mind-bending formulae and long lists which would defy any memory. It has almost come to the point that no one would think of giving a live presentation without the supporting technology to display the relevant information and arguments on a carefully provided screen. We hardly dare speak without the written word to back us up. But this dependence on the written word has an effect on the way we communicate; it shapes the words we use and how we express ourselves. The written word has many strengths, but there are a number of things it cannot do, and we forget them at our peril.

The suggestion that Mark's Gospel is an oral work is not lightly made. We are bound to touch on style, content, the way the Gospel is put together, and even the use the other Gospel-writers seem to have made of the material we find in this Gospel. But the oral depends on a speaker, an audience and an occasion which has brought them together. So often the effectiveness of the spoken word depends on the skills of the speaker and his ability to use the tools at his disposal. Pace of delivery, tone of voice, eye-contact – non-verbal communication – and the general circumstances of the moment all contribute to the effectiveness of the presentation, the way the spoken word is received, and the response it provokes. Yet none of this can be annotated or recorded, and so is lost as soon as the spoken word hits the page.

The Gospels have come down to us as documents, but it is inevitable that in the very first days 'gospelling' – actively sharing the news of Jesus and inviting others to come to faith in him – must have started with the oral. No one doubts that. On the most human level, person to person, experiences were shared, stories told, convictions expressed which would have carried all the passion of those who had discovered their lives changed by their new-found faith in Jesus. This form of communication could not have been more direct and uncomplicated – and it was all the more powerful for that. Rarely would this have happened in speeches or sermons, as we read in the Acts of the Apostles; more often, small groups and individuals would have had the good news of Jesus shared with them, and this would have been done, not by a few specialists, but by ordinary members of the Church who had a story to tell. Always that story was of Jesus; often the stories were told in a way that reflected what it meant to the people who experienced him – their response was part of the story and shaped the way it was told. But because the story was of Jesus, each 'telling' was more than just the personal reminiscences of an individual: it was the 'Jesus story' which belonged to the whole community. It was a story that was told many times, and gradually this repetition would have begun to shape the way it was done, the phrases used and particular points stressed. It is the nature of the oral to retain flexibility, and this enables it to discover ways of expressing things which sharpen and clarify the message given. Usually, the fewer words used, the more powerful the impact; so while the stories were being repeated, they were also being honed, extraneous matters were dropped and thus the picture being presented became ever clearer and shorter. Even when this informal editing process has gone as far as it can without losing anything essential to the story, the oral retains its natural flexibility. Not so with the written word: once it is written, it becomes set, as in stone. Those who pass it on have particular words to use. This instils a disciplined way of passing on information, which has its uses in bringing a certain consistency to the material, but the nature of that material has changed because there is no longer any room for flexibility.

Something else has changed as well. The oral is at its best when it is engaging people; it is a very personal way of communicating. In particular it has the power to touch hearts as well as minds, to provoke a response from its audience because they are caught up in the drama which is being presented in words. The change from oral to written changes the nature of the relationship from speaker and audience to writer and reader; it puts distance between the reader and the drama being presented; the tendency is to inform rather than engage. In the wake of this change, other kinds of material become necessary – explanations and editorial comment especially, which fill the gaps inevitably created.

Both the oral and the written word are part of the process which has brought us our Gospels, and they both have their place in the growing, changing life of the young Church. While 'gospelling' must have started with the oral, there came a time (rather later on) when the needs of the Church were bound to require written works which could act as the core documents for all Christians. At the point when the oral became written, it is entirely likely that fresh material was included which did not have the same oral pedigree. The temptation to do this must have been overwhelming, especially bearing in mind some of the natural weaknesses of the oral pattern. In the oral, lists are anathema; passages such as instructions or a series of commands are out of place, but such material became more and more important as the years went by.

What we shall find, as we examine St Mark's Gospel, is that the natural features of oral tradition – brevity, flexibility, continuity, directness and the ability to engage an audience – are to be found in plenty, and this contrasts with the styles of both Matthew and Luke which bear all the hallmarks of the written word. What is particularly unexpected is to discover that what confirms its oral nature is the way both Matthew and Luke use the material we are familiar with from Mark's Gospel. We have observed that the oral retains a natural flexibility as long as it is oral; once written down the flexibility disappears. If Mark had already been written down when Matthew and Luke began their Gospels, they too would have been constrained in the use of that material, because it already had a form which discouraged others playing fast and loose with it. The widely held expectation is that we would find very considerable verbal agreement between the different Gospels. In fact, both Matthew and Luke, even when they are recording material found in Mark's Gospel, make wholesale changes almost routinely. There are only two verses which, in the Greek, are identical in all three Gospels. One of them is a quotation from Isaiah (Mark 1:3); the other is a saying which may well have been a quotation from another source (Mark 10:31). Neither Matthew nor

Luke has treated Mark's text as if it was already written down.

The brief general outline I have given of the beginning of 'gospelling' can do no more than suggest a possible way in which the whole process developed. There will almost certainly have been many ways in which the Church shared its good news, but perhaps it is possible to see that in the natural process of sharing their experience and telling people about Jesus we find the origins of the Gospels we have. The first Christians discovered that it was not arguments and proofs which touched the hearts and brought people to faith, but the actions of Jesus and what they meant to his disciples which were the winning combination. This is what we find in St Mark's Gospel. It may well be that in this Gospel we have one way Christians used of presenting Jesus, one way of many, but a way which endured and was widely used in many parts of the Church. As such both Matthew and Luke would have been aware of it as an oral tradition, just one source of material among others, as they set about writing their very different Gospels.

With this general background in mind, we must now turn to examine St Mark's Gospel, and listen to the clues the text gives us of its true purpose and meaning.

A Journey through the Gospel of Mark

'The beginning of the gospel of Jesus Christ the Son of God. In the prophet Isaiah it stands written: I am sending my herald ahead of you; he will prepare your way.' (Mark 1:1 and 2)

Every commentator on the Gospels will be aware that it is the Gospel which is of primary importance; words about the Gospels must take second place to the Gospels themselves. What follows, therefore, is intended to do no more than help us to see more clearly what is in front of us.

In the last chapter, we explored the opening words of the Gospel. They are extraordinarily brief, and yet they tell us almost everything we need to know about the Gospel which follows. This Gospel is not just about Jesus: he is the good news, because as the story unfolds we will be brought to those moments when Jesus is acknowledged to be *'Christ'* (Messiah) (Mark 8:29) and *'Son of God.'* (Mark 15:39), and as Christ and Son of God he has come to fulfil all God's promises and set God's people free from the burden and curse of sin and death. What looks like a headline is also telling us where the storyline will take us, and introduces us to one of the features of this Gospel, its connectedness – one phrase or episode leading us on to the next, and holding the whole work together as a continuous whole. There are few explanations or editorial comments; nothing must be allowed to intrude on the flow of the presentation; everything we need to know is included in the story itself.

We noted earlier that there was no literary form to the way this Gospel begins: its authors have not needed the help of any of the conventional ways of beginning a story. We have seen how both Matthew and Luke have used patterns already widely used elsewhere to give them a start. No such help is necessary for Mark. The setting in which these words are spoken gives the starting point; there is no need for a framework of words when speaker and audience face each other. This makes sense of the very open beginning we are given, and helps us to understand the directness and the brevity for which this Gospel as a whole is renowned.

The starting-point for the drama of this Gospel is the words of the prophets. Great play is often made of the fact that the first words from the prophets are quoted from Malachi, not Isaiah as Mark 1:2 suggests. It is a minor academic point; the authors' purpose in quoting the prophets was to emphasise that the story which is about to unfold is to be understood within the context of God's promises of old to his Chosen People. He promised a 'herald' to go ahead of the person he was sending; his task was to prepare people for the coming of the Chosen One; he is to proclaim his message 'in the wilderness;' the One who is to come is 'the Lord.'

It was in fulfilment of these prophetic words that John came; they give us the context in which John's ministry is to be understood. Mark's record of John's ministry is the briefest possible: even the description of John's clothing and diet is not a throwaway biographical note; it identifies John as the promised Elijah.

Last but not least in this opening passage, which is leading up to the appearance of Jesus, are the surprising words, 'he will baptize you with the Holy Spirit.' (Mark 1:8) It is almost as if the speaker has forgotten himself for a moment, and speaks to the audience directly about what will happen if they come to believe in Jesus and commit themselves to follow him. It is a sentence which only makes sense in the life of the Church, and in particular when the people being addressed are not yet believers or members of the Church.

We have been well prepared for the appearance of Jesus. In a very matter-of-fact way we are told where he came from and that he was baptized by John — the storyline is underway. But there is nothing ordinary about what happened: the descent of the Spirit and the voice from heaven identify Jesus as the promised 'Lord' who is to come — the loved Son who is equipped with God's power and has his blessing (Mark 1:10 and 11), and it is as the empowered Son of God that Jesus confronts the Tempter in the place that was thought to be his stronghold; it is portrayed as a battle; the evil one is confronted by the One who is wholly good (a foretaste of things to come).

In thirteen short verses Mark has opened his Gospel, given us the necessary background, introduced Jesus and left us in no doubt as to who he is and what he has come to do – a remarkable beginning which has also introduced us to many of the features of this Gospel: its brevity is breathtaking; the connectedness between the different elements of the introduction (the words of the prophets, John's ministry and message, Jesus' arrival and identity, even the audience itself) is intense; no explanations are given because everything is included in the way the introduction is told. This is the style of Mark in a nutshell.

But the time has come to move on, and the storyline closes the introductions with the note of John's arrest. This is not just a recalling something that happened; our attention is turned to Jesus and his ministry which lies ahead. And there is a change here too. Everything up to this point has looked to the future; Jesus' proclamation is in the present: *The time has arrived; the kingdom of God is upon you. Repent, and believe the good news.'* (Mark 1:15)

With this, the action begins. There is a succession of events, briefly told, around the Sea of Galilee; the Sea will be the general background of so much that happens in the first half of the Gospel, and it is not very surprising that the first people Jesus calls are fishermen. It seems that everything Jesus touches, he changes – lives, sickness, teaching, even the grip of evil spirits. The whole storyline has a feeling of urgency about it, and where the link between one event and another is difficult, the phrase *'and immediately'* bridges any gap and keeps the sense of urgency alive.

The first event of any substance is the account of Jesus teaching and healing in the synagogue at Capernaum (Mark 1:21-28), but the event tells us more than simply what happened in the synagogue that Sabbath. The message for us who hear this Gospel is in the responses of the people, who manage to comment on both his teaching and his act of healing: *'He speaks with authority. When he gives orders, even the unclean spirits obey.'*

What begins on a local and domestic level soon grows, and over the next few chapters the scale of what Jesus does and the responses of the people increase. In the best storytelling tradition the whole presentation develops, and we are carried along by a storyline which does not flag. The responses are not always of wonder and amazement. Very soon there is criticism and opposition, but each occasion tells us more about Jesus and helps us to understand the meaning of what he is doing. So, in the healing of the paralysed man (Mark 2:1-12) we not only have the response of the crowd – *'Never before have we seen anything like this'* – but startling words which underline the meaning of Jesus' action, *'But to convince you that the Son of Man has authority on earth to forgive sins.'* This pattern is repeated in the next event – the call of Levi when Jesus is on his way down to the sea where he teaches the people, and the celebratory meal which follows. His invitation of Levi is as much part of his campaign against evil and sin as are his healings – *'I did not come to call the virtuous, but sinners'* (Mark 2:17), and when he is challenged by the Pharisees because his followers are not doing what other religious groups are doing, Jesus emphasises that with his coming everything is changing; the old patterns are being superseded – *'New wine goes into fresh skins.'* (Mark 2:22).

Of all the issues that will have been contentious between the Jewish community and the young Church it is the question of the Sabbath. It produced the deepest conflicts, so it is not surprising that it features at this point, when the changing order of things is in the air. Two events bring it to a head, the plucking of the ears of corn by the disciples (Mark 2:23-28) and the healing of the man with the withered arm (Mark 3:1-6). Once again, it is Jesus' reply to the accusation which puts the event in a new perspective. Jesus refers his accusers to the revered King David whose action in eating the sacred bread contravened the rules. What the disciples did was no different, so are they condemning King David? But the mere mention of David has messianic undertones; Jesus as Messiah has the authority to use the Sabbath as God would want, and his final answer puts the matter in a new way: *'The Sabbath was made for the sake of man, not man for the Sabbath; so the Son of Man is lord even of the Sabbath.'* (Mark 2:27 and 28)

But the Sabbath controversies are not over. Jesus restores a man's withered arm at a synagogue one Sabbath. It was a confrontation waiting to happen, and Jesus is more than ready to face his critics with the true nature of things – *'Is it permitted to do good or to do evil on the Sabbath, to save life or to kill?'* (Mark 3:4). If we think Jesus is rather overstating it, the end of the story sets the record straight: Jesus has given back to the man his ability to work, support his family, live a full life; his critics got into a huddle with the aim *'to bring about Jesus' death.'* (Mark 3:6)

Jesus and his disciples once again go down to the sea, the place where Jesus has so often been portrayed as meeting the people's needs. The crowd which gathers because of what they have heard about Jesus seems to have come from far and wide, and it is not surprising that soon enough he is healing and driving out evil spirits; it is a sign of people's needs that the situation might well have proved overwhelming, so there is a boat set aside in readiness. They may simply have come because of their own need, but Jesus is looking beyond that, and chooses this moment to enrol a core group who will be with him and take their part in the great campaign. The disciples are named - this is one of the few lists included in this Gospel (it may have been inserted later, when the Gospel was being written down). From now on, the disciples take their place in the story, not only as Jesus' companions, but also as those who put questions to Jesus, giving a framework for the authors to include further material.

Every storyteller has moments when their links are a bit contrived; this is one of them. Jesus was in the hill country to call the disciples; now he is in a house, surrounded by so many people that ordinary patterns of life are impossible. On the one hand there is popularity, on the other concern from his family that he needs rescuing from himself; faith and disbelief are placed in close proximity, and the nature of disbelief is examined when seen side by side with faith. Legal experts from Jerusalem, no less, give their explanation for what he is doing, but they are no match for Jesus' frank logic, and cannot hide the true nature of the stance they take. The arrival of his family (who were only doing what families were supposed to do – looking after their own when things were going wrong) provides the setting for a saying of Jesus which will have had strong resonance with the earliest Christians: *'Whoever does the will of God is my brother and sister and mother.'* (Mark 3:35)

Up to this point, we have been told frequently of Jesus preaching and teaching, but we have not experienced Jesus the teacher at work. Chapter 4 puts this right. On the surface, at least, the parable of the sower seems a most unlikely place to start, but it is important not to take this one parable in isolation. Verses 3-34 belong together, and together they have a common message which is as much for the people listening to the Gospel being presented as it is for the people to whom Christ spoke. The challenge to both is to respond to Jesus and what he says with faith. His *'If you have ears to hear, then hear'* comes not only at the end of the parable but later in the chapter as well (Mark 4:9 and 23). Parables demand that the listener looks for the meaning in the story – and the point of parables is not to disguise the truth but reveal it – but it is only faith that discerns the message Jesus is giving, and it is only those who look with faith and commit themselves to it who will discover the riches of God's promises. The authors have not forgotten why they are telling the story of Jesus: it is so that those who hear will come to discipleship and the full life Jesus brings.

The link between Jesus teaching the crowd and the next event is not difficult. Jesus is already in a boat which naturally enough leads on to the suggestion to cross over to the other side of the sea. But there could hardly be a greater contrast between the idyllic scene of Jesus teaching the people from the boat and a storm putting all their lives in danger. The stilling of the storm presents an entirely different challenge to the disciples, and demands that they face questions of a completely different order: *'Who can this be? Even the wind and the sea obey him.'* (Mark 4:41) For Jesus to be healer and teacher is one thing; for him to quell the storm with a simple word of command is another. What made them fear for their lives (and fishermen would have known when they were in real danger) Jesus masters. The question the disciples ask themselves is precisely the question the authors want to put in front of their audience (and it was all the more powerful because the question is left in the air for the audience to answer for themselves).

At this point there is a change of focus in this Gospel. From presenting Jesus doing remarkable things, increasingly the audience is being challenged to respond with faith to the Jesus who is being shown them. The stilling of the storm is followed by the driving out of a particularly strong demon (Mark 5:1-20), and afterwards by the story of Jesus bringing a young girl back to life (Mark 5:21-43). Remarkable events, but both told in a way that sheds light on how this Gospel is constructed, and the messages the authors were looking to convey. In order to give a proper picture of the healing of 'Legion' the audience needs to know a great deal about his condition. This is done by description in the course of telling the story rather than information and explanations; the introduction to the story is constructed with great care in order to do this. The responses to the healing are significant: the people of the area are afraid and ask Jesus to leave; such power is disturbing, and in view of the loss they have incurred they want nothing to do with Jesus. But their response is also a sign of unbelief (not so different from the disciples at the stilling of the storm) and they push Jesus away from them because he represents something they do not understand. The story, however, does not end until we are told how the people of the Ten Towns respond to what the healed man told them – *'and everyone was amazed'* (Mark 5:20). The audience listening to the Gospel is to be astonished, and to reflect on the power and the compassion of Jesus in restoring this very disturbed person.

Power and compassion are also the marks of the next event, but while faith and fear were contrasted in the previous story, Jesus' words to Jairus – *'Do not be afraid; simply have faith'* (Mark 5:36) underline what faith makes possible. In this story, the authors have made the most of its potential for drama. It begins with a surprise – the leader of a synagogue asks Jesus for help, the request springing from the understandable agony of a father whose daughter is at death's door. Jesus goes with him to his house accompanied by a great crowd. But this takes time, so another story is included which gives the sense of time passing. The crowd acts as cover for a woman who had suffered for a dozen years; no one had been able to help her, no matter what the doctors had prescribed. It is her secret approach and her unspoken request which halts their progress. The disciples cannot see what the fuss was all about; Jesus knew very well. Someone who has suffered a terrible stigma has approached him. She needs healing for her condition, and release from the prison of guilt and shame at what she has had to go through. When Jesus asks *'Who touched my clothes?'* (Mark 5:30) the healing has already happened; it is in her open acknowledgement of what she has done that she is also set free from her prison. Jesus' gentle words underline the importance of her faith; this is the very quality Jairus must have when the message comes from his house that the girl has died. At this Jesus takes charge; he tells Jairus to believe (even though he could not possibly know how it would help); he allows only three of his followers to accompany him, and they come to the house where the mourners are already raising a dirge. Again, he asserts his authority; he puts the professional mourners out, takes the girl's parents and his companions and goes to the child. His words to her are simple – like waking a child from sleep – and she proves that she is alive by getting up and walking about. The parents are overjoyed – but bringing the girl back to life must not be the end of it. To many people's surprise Jesus tells the parents that they must tell no one. Why? They must have been bursting to shout it from the housetops! Jesus has given the girl her life back; he wants her to live it to the full. She will never be able to do that if she is always 'the girl who came back from the dead.' Like the woman before her, the girl also needs both to be restored, and to be completely freed from all the superstition and voyeurism which surely would follow such an episode.

It is worth dwelling on these stories; here is storytelling at its very best. In describing the plot (omitting quite a few details on the way) I have used far more words than Mark has in telling the stories in full. My explanations are far less colourful or vivid, and add nothing to what we are told – at points I have hardly done the stories themselves justice. It is in story form that we are enabled to perceive the love, sensitivity and compassion of Christ; his power to heal what had defeated others, and to bring someone back from the dead challenges every listener to want the faith that makes it possible for Christ to do this for them. Neither illness nor death is all-powerful when confronted with the power of Christ.

It is part of the art of the oral to allow the storyline to contain contrasts which sharpen the significance of the different elements of the story. After such stories as we have just heard – setting before us the power of Christ and challenging each listener to come to faith – we are now presented with an event where faith is lacking. Jesus visits his home town, and even preaches in the synagogue – but there was no faith. They ask all the right questions; they know about what he had done elsewhere, but it was just too much for the people he grew up with to think of him as anything more than one of them. Their lack of faith limits what Jesus can do, and what he can be to them. It must have been a sobering visit. (Mark 6:1-6)

Jesus' response is to launch a mission, and for the first time we hear of the disciples taking an active part. His instructions to them carry all the signs of urgency. They go with a message, the need for radical change, but Jesus knows that their reception will be mixed, and he tells them how to respond when they face rejection or indifference. For they go, not as themselves but as representatives of Christ, proclaiming his message.

We might think it strange that in so short a Gospel there is room for the unedifying episode of court intrigue which follows, but it has more than one function. The introduction to the story keeps the question of who Jesus is in the mind of the audience. All the suggestions were wide of the mark, yet all seem to sense that in some way this strange preacher was 'of God.' It also tells of the death of John the Baptist, a sad story, but one which succeeded in showing the kind of motives which led to the callous execution of this great man.

As in the last chapter, parts of one event (the mission of the disciples) are placed either side of a seemingly unrelated story, perhaps to help the audience feel that time is passing. If they have one thing in common it is the unbelief the disciples will encounter, and the unbelief of Herod. Whether or not we see significance in that, we need now to prepare for another sudden change. Two events follow, and Mark quite deliberately places them together. They are remarkable events in every way, but they also seem to echo great events in Israel's formative life, and point forward to the life of the Church. It is difficult not to believe that those telling the stories did not see the crossing of the Red Sea on foot and the feeding of the people with manna in the desert in the story of Jesus feeding the five thousand and walking on the water. Phrases such as *'because they were like sheep without a shepherd'* (Mark 6:34) and *'This is a remote* (some translations have 'desert') *place'* (Mark 6:35) could well have had this further reference as the story took shape. In the same way, for every Christian the 'breaking of bread' and the reference to water may also hold echoes of the Eucharist and Baptism.

These events have considerable importance in the unfolding of the presentation of Jesus in this Gospel. Jesus takes up the role of shepherd – feeding the people by his teaching before feeding them miraculously with five loaves and two fishes. Through his actions the needs of this huge crowd are met – and to spare. In coming to the disciples, walking on the water, he is not only meeting their needs as they struggle against a fierce headwind; he also confronts the disciples who seem to have learned nothing from the experience of the feeding. What so easily could go unnoticed in this account is that there is no response, either of amazement or puzzlement, at the extraordinary feeding. As Mark puts it: *'At this they were utterly astounded, for they had not understood the incident of the loaves; their minds were closed.'* (Mark 6:51 and 52) This is unfinished business which will soon be revisited.

The normal pattern of the campaign resumes, and Mark gives us a very general picture of the ministry as Jesus goes from place to place. Into this general picture an encounter is inserted which sits rather uncomfortably in such a setting. It is always trouble when officials from Jerusalem are mentioned; this is no exception. The accusation is about rules and regulations and the traditional way of doing things. Undoubtedly, the Jews and the young Church clashed violently over dietary laws and related matters – that is the setting to which this story belongs, not the bringing to faith of those who are enquiring about Jesus. Jesus' response fits such a confrontation, and the editorial comment *'By saying this he declared all foods clean'* (Mark 7:9) is wholly out of place in this Gospel, as is the list with which this episode ends. This may well be an incident added to the text as it was being written down.

Suddenly, things are back on track again, although Jesus and the disciples are in Gentile territory (Mark 7:24). It is a Gentile woman, who seeks him out, but she is not daunted by the barriers that exist between Jews and Gentiles, and Jesus does not refuse her. The conversation between them is widely misunderstood: it is often thought that Jesus is resisting her advances; more likely is the possibility that Jesus recognises her faith (and she his readiness to respond) and they share a joke at the stupidity of the way Jews call the Gentiles 'dogs' but their own people 'children.' Another healing follows; those involved in bringing the man to Jesus cannot contain themselves, despite Jesus' instructions. But the storyline presses on; the drive is to get back to the question of the feeding. The account of this feeding (of the four thousand) has some small differences from the earlier feeding. On this occasion too there is no response on the part of the disciples. But then we notice a pattern repeating itself: they cross the lake; Pharisees question him: *'To test him they asked him for a sign from heaven.'* (Mark 8:11). After the extraordinary sign of feeding thousands of people to ask for a sign seems absurd. Then Jesus and the disciples set out across the lake aware that they are rather short of supplies. The conversation that follows feels both strained and contrived. Jesus is trying to help the disciples come to some understanding of what they have experienced, but it is hard going. They seem so far from realising the true significance of what was happening before their eyes. In reality, Mark is talking to the audience listening to the Gospel being spoken. They need to understand what they have heard before the story comes to the great moment at Caesarea Philippi.

The agonising journey is followed by another healing – but a particularly unusual one: Jesus restores a man's sight gradually (Mark 8:22-26). As we hear the story, its significance is not obvious, but when the next episode as they walked to Caesarea Philippi is related we realise we are being helped to see what is happening (not by explanations but through the drama of story). The blindness of the disciples will give way to partial sight; seeing clearly must wait until Jesus has completed his work.

Jesus now puts the central question of the whole Gospel to the disciples. We have heard echoes of it after the stilling of the storm and in Herod's response to what he had heard about Jesus. It has been felt indirectly as each miracle has been recounted, and each act of compassion touched the lives of those who came to him. But this is altogether more direct and it follows Jesus' struggles to let light into the disciples' closed minds. Jesus asks, *'And you, who do you say I am?'* (Mark 8:29) It comes as something of a surprise that Peter is equally direct: *'You are the Messiah.'* It is a momentous statement. Jesus is the One promised by God; he is the King, the Son of David, who would reign over the promised kingdom. Jesus is the culmination of centuries of waiting, and they are living in the age God had promised. This is the moment to which the whole of the first half of the Gospel has been leading us. At last there is a glimmer of faith, and the authors are hoping that their audience is able to echo Peter's words of faith.

What Peter has discovered is right – but not quite right (like the blind man seeing, but not accurately) – so Jesus sets about correcting him and the other disciples. They have much to learn about what kind of Messiah he is to be. What they expect is the common misconception – a creation of the devil – and Jesus does not mince his words. He makes it clear that his destiny is to: *'endure great suffering, and to be rejected by the elders, chief priests and scribes; to be put to death, and to rise again three days afterwards.'* (Mark 8:30) But Messiah he is, and his purpose is to bring about the kingdom and the freedom which belongs to everyone in that kingdom. So he gathers, not only his disciples, but people beyond the inner circle, and issues a challenge to anyone who wants to follow him: *'Anyone who wants to be a follower of mine must renounce self; he must take up his cross and follow me. Whoever wants to preserve his life will lose it, but whoever is willing to give his life for my sake and for the sake of the Gospel – he will save it. Where is the profit in gaining the whole world at the cost of your own soul? What can you give in exchange for your soul? If anyone disowns me and my teaching in this wicked and sinful generation, the Son of Man will disown when he comes in the glory of the Father with his holy angels. I tell you most solemnly, there are some standing here who will not experience death before they see the kingdom of God come with power.'* (Mark 8:34 to 9:1)

This passage is utterly unique in this Gospel. Jesus is not talking in parables; he is addressing his followers as the newly proclaimed Messiah. It is a message for all generations, and in many ways it is more fitted to the life of the Church than it is to any point in the mission and ministry of Jesus. The necessity for the Messiah to suffer and to die is matched by Jesus' call for the disciple to be ready to take the same path. The challenge has several startling features. The call to 'renounce self' (however it is translated) talks in terms we have not seen before. Fear and self-preservation will always win the day unless love of Christ and faith in him are the real driving forces in their lives. While 'self' is the prime mover in our actions, there will always be a weakness which will undermine discipleship. Peter had to learn this lesson (Mark 14:72) and so did the earliest Christians. Behind the shock of the first command is the understanding that without love of Christ and belief in him being pre-eminent, the disciple will not have the freedom to follow when living out the faith in the harsh realities of the world.

The reference to a cross before the crucifixion has taken place could not possibly have carried the force or meaning during Jesus' life that it did after his death and resurrection. To the disciples it could only have been a puzzle, but on the lips of Christians these words would have carried the full meaning – not only suffering with Christ, but also sharing his victory – and making their identification with Christ in the waters of Baptism. The terrible warnings Jesus gives to those who disown him are hardly a reality for the disciples, but they come into their own in the life of the early Church. These words are placed at this pivotal moment in the Gospel because, for the earliest Christians, this was what faced so many who did make the commitment of faith. In these five verses (Mark 8:34 to 9:1) the message and mission of Jesus is set aside, and those who are called to faith by the proclamation of the Gospel are faced with the cost of discipleship. To us, so many centuries later, it sounds utterly daunting, but it is the nature of love and faith to accept and face such difficulties for the honour of saying, 'I am his disciple.'

The Journey to the Cross

After the pivotal moment at Caesarea Philippi, almost everything changes. Instead of centring his mission around the Sea of Galilee, Jesus and his disciples begin a journey which will bring them to Jerusalem and the living out of the prophecy Jesus has made. From the beginning, Jesus deliberately makes time to be with the disciples. The great stream of miracles comes to an end; there are only two in the chapters that lie ahead, and both of these, like the gradual healing of the blind man, have another significance attached to them by the way they are recorded. Jesus is with the disciples in order to teach them, and much of the teaching sets a new standard which his disciples are to follow. Fundamental approaches to power, money, marriage and faith are all included, each being prompted by an incident or a question. In chapters 9 and 10 each episode is introduced with a reference to the journey and where they have reached.

But before the journey begins, there is another moment when the veil is drawn back, and we are given a glimpse of the hidden glory of Christ. Once again, just the inner circle of three is chosen; once again, they are on a mountain top, the place where Moses of old went to commune with God. The change in Jesus' appearance, the presence of Elijah and Moses, and even the cloud all speak of a moment of revelation. It stands at the beginning of the second half of the Gospel much as the Baptism of Jesus did before the beginning of Jesus' ministry, and again there was a voice, on this occasion heard by the disciples to whom it was addressed: *'This is my Son, my beloved Son; listen to him.'* How much they still have to learn and understand – but they are to be in no doubt about the authority of their master and teacher.

When Jesus and the three return to the others, they are met by a scene of conflict and confusion, but the return is not recorded as we might expect. *'As soon as they saw Jesus the whole crowd were overcome with awe and ran forward to welcome him.'* (Mark 9:15) This description suggests that the young Church saw this moment very much in terms of the Old Testament picture of Moses returning to the people (and commotion greeted him too) after communing with God. The source of confusion was the inability of the disciples to cure a young boy who had been brought to them – and the legal experts were making the most of it. The subtext in the telling of this story is their failure in faith – and where there is a lack of faith there is also impotence – and this is underlined both by Jesus' response – *'What an unbelieving generation!'* – by the impassioned plea of the father – *'I believe; help my unbelief'* and Jesus' explanation to the disciples,

'This kind cannot be driven out except by prayer' (Mark 9:29). Jesus heals the boy and restores him to his father, but this has been the first lesson for the disciples to learn about discipleship: nothing can be attempted without faith.

Now the journey can begin, and the difference between the ministry in Galilee and the journey south to Jerusalem is emphasised. Jesus deliberately chooses to spend much of the time alone with his disciples, teaching them, so we can expect that there will be teaching for those listening to the Gospel in the next few chapters. The beginning of the journey is accompanied by the second of three prophecies Jesus makes about his destiny. It is briefer than the first, but contains the same elements: the necessity for Jesus to be rejected, that he will die and rise again after three days.

A note of the progress they are making introduces another episode – the first of Jesus' directions to his followers on how power should be used among them. Jesus uses a child to illustrate his point. For the Jews of his day, a child has no standing and no authority because he is a child. It is only if they are prepared to follow such a model that they will be fit to be Christ's (and God's) representative. We are, however, at the beginning of a short passage which is held together more by word association than by logic. Anyone today writing the final verses of this chapter would have expressed it very differently. As it is, we have to juggle a confusing set of messages around representatives, children, reward, causes for stumbling and finally salt. It seems that a number of sayings by Jesus, probably made on different occasions, have been brought together, and the verbal links have provided the glue which give us this rather unlikely passage.

Chapter 10 begins with another note of the journey's progress, and for a moment the former pattern of ministry resumes, but this is largely to allow further items of teaching to be presented. The Christian community will inevitably have its differences from other faith groups and the world around. Marriage and divorce are one of the areas in which a different standard is applied. Jesus' answer to the trick question about divorce could hardly have been more orthodox, but it is when he is on his own with the disciples that a difference with Jewish practice suggests itself. Among Jews, a woman did not have the right to divorce her husband; Jesus applies his teaching to both men and women alike.

Another small incident is the occasion for a further bit of teaching. The disciples may have thought they were doing the right thing – protecting Jesus from the clamour of people wanting his time and attention – but that is not Jesus' way, and he makes himself available to welcome and bless the children who are brought to him. The general lesson goes further: all of us need to be brought to Christ; we can only take our place in the kingdom if we are prepared to receive it (Mark 10:13-16).

It is precisely this boon which is the concern of a stranger who approached Jesus as they are once again setting out on the journey – *'Good teacher, what must I do to win eternal life?'* (Mark 10:17). The real teaching for the disciples and those who take up the faith is to be found in Jesus' conversation with the disciples. The incident itself is about discipleship. The man, however genuine, is utterly imprisoned by his wealth; he is not free to pursue the far greater goal of eternal life because he is so caught up with the demands of his present existence. *'Go, sell everything you have'* is really only a preliminary to the nub of their conversation: *'then come and follow me.'* The answer to his original request is that in discipleship and in following Jesus is the way to eternal life. The invitation is offered in love, and Jesus knows how hard it will be for a man who is so imprisoned by his wealth to make the necessary response.

It is this terrible dilemma Jesus shares with his disciples, but he has an opportunity to say to them what was never possible to share with the rich stranger: discipleship has a cost – material, social, and personal – but in discipleship a person receives far more than he gives up. He might even have said that a person is only ready to receive when he has had the courage first to give – in this way the usual expectations in life are turned upside down: *'Many who are first will be last, and the last first.'* (Mark 10:31).

The last of the prophecies is more detailed and is prefaced by deepening apprehension on the part of the disciples. For the first time the occupying power is mentioned, and what Jesus must suffer at the hands of the Romans is spelled out in more detail. As with the previous prophecy, the subject of position and power again presents itself. James and John make a bid for the most important positions when the kingdom comes. Jesus' response is much more detailed. The 'cup' and the 'baptism' will have had a far greater resonance in the life of the Church than when they were spoken by Jesus, but his instruction is clear. They are to follow his example – not the patterns of power and authority which they find in the world around them. He comes to serve, and to bring freedom to many by his self-giving.

The journey is nearing its end. The last significant place before Jerusalem is Jericho, and there the final encounter of the journey takes place. A blind beggar attracts Jesus' attention and has his sight restored. His response is to *'follow Jesus in the way'* – all of which may well have another meaning. This is only the second miracle since Jesus started out towards Jerusalem. Jesus has worked hard to help the disciples see who he is and understand what following him means. Bartimaeus has his sight restored and follows Jesus in 'the way' (one of the earliest ways of talking about the Christian faith). The pun may well be intentional and is the reason why the story is included at this point. But Bartimaeus calls Jesus *'Son of David'* and very soon it will be as 'Son of David', the king promised by God, that Jesus will ride into his capital city.

The Jerusalem Ministry

St Mark's Gospel does not tell of Jesus going to Jerusalem before this moment. When he comes now, it is as the Messiah, the Son of David whose kingdom God had promised many centuries before. That, at least, is the message of this Gospel, and the manner of his arrival at Jerusalem sends precisely this message to those who observed it. From beginning to end, Jesus is very much in charge. It is his choice to ride a donkey – to ride is the action of a king entering his capital; to ride a donkey is to fulfil the words of the prophet Zechariah: *'humble and riding on a donkey'* (Zechariah 9:9), so God's will and purpose lies behind this moment. The people respond in kind – by laying their cloaks and leaves on the road they are welcoming their king. Their words ring with messianic hope; the message of the moment, as Mark records it, could hardly be plainer.

The saddest possible contrast to the enthusiasm of the 'people's' shouts is to be found in the Temple. It was business as usual, not a ripple disturbing the surface of its normal life. There is no welcome, no response, not even a glimmer of recognition. Jesus observes this, before leaving the city and going out to Bethany with his disciples. His response to this failure will be felt the next day.

The craft of storytelling not only involves painting pictures in words which can stay in the mind. The best stories have development; they often operate on more than one level, and so present each episode at its proper place in the growing drama. Mark's presentation of Jesus' ministry in Jerusalem is storytelling at its best. There are the events – dramatic enough by any standard, but there are also the undercurrents which rumble in the background – increasing opposition which time and again breaks out in arguments and clashes. In the course of the three chapters 11 to 13, Jesus sets the Temple to rights, answers criticisms levelled at him, and establishes himself as the supreme interpreter of scripture with an authority no one can match. Finally, he moves beyond the Temple and other present concerns to the culmination of all things, encouraging his disciples to remain faithful in all the suffering they will have to undergo. The broad sweep of these chapters brings its listeners to see in Jesus a teacher with matchless authority, and the One who can speak about the end times with knowledge and understanding. Each episode in Jesus' Jerusalem ministry has its place in the developing drama, and should not be taken in isolation.

That is particularly true of the next episode – the cursing of the fig tree (Mark 11:12-14; 20-25). This curious action is placed either side of Jesus' action in the Temple – deliberately so, and should not be taken out of that context. Very consciously, it is a comment on the Temple and its failure to recognise Jesus as the promised Messiah, despite the way Jesus entered the city and the words of the people. The fate of the fig tree speaks of the terrible results which will flow from the blindness of the Temple authorities to what God is doing. The clue for taking it in this way is to be found in the words *'for it was not the season for figs'* (verse 13); Jesus does not expect there to be any fruit; it is an acted parable. Jesus' action in the Temple has all the hallmarks of prophetic action, such as the great prophets of old had undertaken. The Temple authorities were better placed than anyone to understand this, but their response was predictably hostile, despite the words of Jesus, *'My house shall be called a house of prayer for all nations.'* (Mark 11:17).

Curiously, the only teaching on prayer this Gospel offers is to be found when Jesus responds to Peter's *'The tree which you cursed has withered.'* (Mark 11:21). It is characteristically pithy, but all the more powerful for that: *'Have faith in God; believe that you have received it and it will be yours; forgive, so that your Father in heaven may forgive you the wrongs you have done.'*

The series of confrontations begins. The first to challenge Jesus are the Temple authorities. Jesus replies with a question (which was the usual way to move a debate forward), but such are the implications of his question that the authorities cannot answer it without incriminating themselves. The listeners would have been able to give their answer from the way the encounter is set out. But the episode is not over. Jesus adds a parable which can have only one meaning to those listening. The authorities are usurpers, false tenants (and murderers at that) and they will be replaced by God. The parable only really works after the crucifixion, since the identification of Jesus with the son of the owner is the missing clue. The context given to the parable makes sure there is only one interpretation, and the final words of the encounter confirm this understanding.

It is then the turn of the Pharisees (with the Herodians). They put to Jesus the kind of question that is intended to leave him nowhere to go, whichever way he answers. But his answer leaves them amazed: *'Pay Caesar what belongs to Caesar, and God what belongs to God.'* (Mark 12:17). The other leading religious party of the day is next to pit their wits against Jesus. Typically for them, they bring up a question about resurrection, based on what Moses had laid down many centuries before. They fare no better than the other parties in their challenge to Jesus, and they receive a crisp reply from Jesus to which they have no answer: *'You know neither the scriptures nor the power of God'* and *'He is not the God of the dead but of the living. You are very far from the truth.'* (Mark 12:24 and 27)

Finally a lawyer comes to him, and invites Jesus to speak of the commandments. His summary of the law draws approval from the lawyer: *'that means far more than any whole-offerings and sacrifices.'* When Jesus has answered all the challenges brought to him, he has challenges of his own, not least about the Messiah, and criticisms, especially of the bogus respectability of the legal experts. Finally, he contrasts the charitable contributions of the well-to-do with the unnoticed generosity of a poor widow.

Anyone hearing Mark's account of these encounters will have had their appreciation of Jesus greatly deepened. It is not that he was clever enough not to get caught out; at each point Jesus gives answers and teaching which has depth and understanding far beyond those who contended with him. He is the teacher supreme, and it is as a teacher who speaks with authority and truth that we are led to his final teaching about the future, and the challenges that his followers are bound to face when they come to believe in him.

Chapter 13 presents problems all of its own. Some commentators have called this chapter 'the little apocalypse' because it borrows the patterns of a particular kind of literature which came into use during difficult periods in Jewish history. Apocalyptic literature is highly symbolic, and was used to encourage believers to keep the faith in the face of overwhelming odds. While it appears to be talking of things to do with the end of the world, those who know the code can interpret what is said in terms of the events they are living through. Its message is: the times are difficult, but God is in charge, and those who keep the faith will be vindicated. Often this kind of literature is put into the mouth of some great figure in the past. After establishing Jesus' authority as the supreme teacher, it is no surprise that the authors of this Gospel make use of the apocalyptic style to give encouragement to the faithful and those who are ready to take up the faith. This chapter also provides the best possible setting in which to tell of the rejection and suffering Jesus faced as he lived out his destiny as Messiah and Saviour.

Although the chapter seems at first to talk about the Temple, this is no more than a link, and the request for a sign introduces the very different patterns of thought which apocalyptic literature uses. The real subject of Jesus' teaching is the dangers and difficulties disciples face. Many of the sufferings described were precisely what some of the faithful had already experienced, but the message of verses 9 to 14 is clear: *'But whoever endures to the end will be saved.'* This points to the future, so the development of the picture which now takes place puts the present suffering into an eternal context, and this reaches its climax in speaking of the end times – very apocalyptic. It might appear that Jesus is talking about distant events; the challenge put by this chapter is very much in the present tense: *'Keep awake.'* (Mark 13:36)

The Passion Narrative

The Passion Narrative (chapters 14 and 15) brings us to the heart of this Gospel. From the way it is set out, it would be a surprise if these chapters with chapter 16 had not often been used separately from the rest of the Gospel. It is in every way self-contained, and has a clarity which suggests that on other occasions it stood on its own, and was not solely used as the final chapters of the Gospel.

It begins by carefully introducing the dramatis personae, the people at the centre of the drama. Each brings an important element to the events which will unfold. First on stage are the chief priests and legal experts who want to get rid of Jesus; then Jesus is presented among friends, but aware that his destiny is in rejection and death. The use of very expensive perfume provokes an argument – largely because the disciples have not understood the nature of what is about to happen. They favour calculated philanthropy; Jesus will live out his destiny in costly self-giving. Finally, Judas, one of the Twelve, plans to betray Jesus to the chief priests, and is to be paid for his trouble. All this is set against the backdrop of Passover, the celebration of God's setting his people free from slavery in Egypt, and the beginning of the journey to the Promised Land. It is the death of the Passover Lamb which enables them to escape the final plague, and they were to eat the meal already dressed and ready to start the long march.

The Passion Narrative is a unity which flows uninterrupted towards its climax. Essentially, it is one story with many different episodes, and anything that does not have a place in the unfolding of the story has been allowed to drop away. On the face of it, we are given a direct account of how it happened. But not far beneath the surface is a commentary on its meaning, so that at every twist and turn we are enabled to see what is happening.

If we are tempted to think of Jesus as the helpless victim, time and again it is Jesus who makes the decisive move. He sends two disciples to prepare for Passover, telling them to look for a man carrying a jar of water (unthinkable! This was women's work). At the meal he reveals that it is *'one of the Twelve'* who will betray him. He breaks the bread and gives the cup, prefiguring his death and speaking of a new covenant which his death will make possible. As they make their way to the Mount of Olives, he tells his disciples that they will stumble because of him, quoting Zechariah 13:7. In the events that are about to unfold, even their failure is predicted. God himself is not aloof; he is closely engaged with every action in the drama. In the Garden of Gethsemane, it is Jesus who leads his disciples out to meet those who are going to arrest him.

Each episode adds something fresh. The astonishing brevity of each story within the great drama tells us how often it has been repeated and paired down to the account we have (a sign of how important it was to them, and how often it was used). The account of the Passover meal takes less than ten verses. Its brevity belies its importance. Jesus not only reveals that it is one of the Twelve who will betray him, but he re-affirms that what lies ahead for him is his destiny set out in scripture (Mark 14:21). No details of the Passover meal are mentioned, though it was for them, as Jews, a most sacred ceremony. Instead we have the briefest account of his initiating a new Passover and covenant, created by his self-giving. He breaks the bread (as his body will be broken) and shares the cup (it is in the shedding of his blood that the new covenant is sealed, so that many will enter into the freedom he came to bring), and by his abstinence he dedicates himself to completing the task laid on him by God.

Traditionally, the Passover meal ends with a hymn, and those keeping the feast are required to spend the night within the greater Jerusalem area. Jesus and his disciples make their way to a garden the other side of the Kidron valley. But we are not told about the walk; what occupies centre stage is Jesus' warning to the disciples that they are going to *'lose faith.'* They protest, none louder than Peter, but their bravado is a sad prelude to what is going to happen. But Jesus puts it in a quite different context: *'I will strike the shepherd and the sheep will be scattered'* (Zechariah 13:7). Their failure is also written in scripture and is within the plan and purposes of God. But just when all seems lost, Jesus looks ahead: *'After I am raised, I shall go ahead of you into Galilee.'* (Mark 14:28) But Peter will not entertain the possibility that he will fail Jesus (as he sees it), only to receive the chilling warning about what will happen: *'before the cock crows twice, you yourself will disown me three times.'*

They go to the garden, ostensibly to spend the night, but Jesus asks his inner circle to keep awake and offer their support as the weight of the events to come bears down upon him. Those listening to Jesus are helped to understand the horror of the moment, and that dread is reflected in the prayer Jesus offers. It is the most direct and intimate of prayers (Mark alone uses the greeting *'Abba,'* a word only used to those with whom a person has the closest personal relationship), yet many of the faithful would have recognised in Jesus' prayer to the Father the outline of the Lord's Prayer which we know from Matthew and Luke. Here Jesus is not confined by a set form of words, but prays it freely, as the situation demands. Three times Jesus comes to the disciples; three times they are asleep, and in this way the isolation he suffers deepens, as the audience is prepared for the arrest. When the moment comes, it is Jesus who leads his disciples out to meet his betrayer and the extraordinary rabble sent to arrest him (is a serving-maid really there?). The betrayal is done with a kiss; the arrest is violent. It is at Jesus' words *But let the scriptures be fulfilled'* that the disciples and all those with Jesus flee, including a young man who only narrowly avoids arrest. But the action is in fulfilment of scripture, within the purposes of God.

It is impossible to call what follows 'a trial.' At best it is a time to gather and test what evidence they have, not a formal trial. It is unthinkable that people with evidence to give would be available at that hour and on Passover night at that. That there are any witnesses at all suggests a certain amount of forward planning – albeit probably at short notice. Yet for the listeners, two things light up proceedings: *'I will pull down this Temple, made with human hands, and in three days I will build another, not made with hands.'* (Mark 14:58). The sting of this quote is in the less obvious meaning of 'made with human hands' – idolatrous. It is when Jesus (verse 62) acknowledges his true identity and destiny that the high priest tears his robes and Jesus is pronounced unanimously to be guilty and should be put to death. This is the moment when the ill-treatment begins.

What happens to Jesus stands in complete contrast to what befalls Peter. In the confusion he had managed to find himself in the high priest's house, albeit below stairs with the slaves and the servants, and very probably with those who had been in the garden to arrest Jesus. He was one of the crowd until he was noticed by a serving-maid who said she recognised him from the garden. The denial may have come easily – certainly it was his fear talking; and although he goes outside there was nothing he could do to prevent the second and the third occasion. It is the cockcrow which brings him to his senses, and the realisation of what he has done brings tears of remorse – a very human moment which the audience would have understood very well. It also provides the kind of contrast which highlights what is going on in the greater drama. Jesus is examined by the highest Jewish authority in the land; Peter is confronted by a chance remark. Jesus is condemned and beaten; not a finger is laid on Peter – yet it is Peter who fails the test.

The trial before Pilate is no more satisfactory, but it is told so skilfully that no amount of explanation would have been able to set out any more clearly both the outward events and the hidden motives. One thing is clear:

Jesus is innocent (and Pilate knows it; at one stage he almost acts as counsel for the defence.) but the whole event is not about innocence and justice; what is being played out is a drama of unbelief and rejection, compromise and self-preservation. The result is inevitable: Jesus is to die. But Pilate does not condemn him; he hands him over (much as an animal is handed over for sacrifice).

The soldiers too have part of the action. Before the tedious and sometimes dangerous duty of supervising an execution, they make sport of their prisoner. It was common practice. But the soldiers' game of 'King' is not told just because it happened; we are told about it because the authors want us to be reminded that Jesus is King to those who believe in him; he has a kingdom for those who will receive it. We are reminded of this before the crucifixion itself, so that as we are caught up in the action at Golgotha, we, the audience, will have in mind that this is happening to the One who really is King.

The account of the crucifixion itself is brief, factual and without emotion. The sentences are short, without colour – almost as if it is too painful to speak about. We are given the name of a witness, who is formally identified; other witnesses watch from a distance. The actions of the soldiers are exactly what everyone in the Roman Empire would have expected – even so the words from Psalm 22 seem to hover behind the record we are given. Even the words of mockery from the bystanders seem to underline the meaning of what is happening. It is because he does not come down from the cross that Jesus is able to save. The words about the Temple, used at his trial, are thrown in his face. Disbelief has found its voice. But then comes the darkness and Jesus' cry of abandonment (words taken from Psalm 22: they express his predicament completely, but it should be noted that the Psalm ends in triumph and in peace.) The darkness speaks its own language and adds a dimension to the moment that explanations cannot.

Jesus dies. At this point almost all that Jesus has prophesied has come about, but this is the moment when two things happen: *the curtain of the Temple was torn in two from top to bottom.'* (Mark 15:38). The Temple can no longer be the focus of God's presence with his people. That now passes to Jesus. It is significant that the moment of his death is chosen to mark the transition – a reminder that for the earliest of believers Jesus' death is supremely important as the moment when he brings to completion the task laid upon him by the Father. It is also the moment when the centurion puts into words the affirmation with which the Gospel began, acknowledging Jesus to be *'Son of God.'*

In one sense, the Gospel is now complete. If the audience has followed the unfolding of the good news of Jesus, they are now in a position to make the same acknowledgement as the centurion: Jesus is both Christ and Son of God. But not even Mark can quite leave it there. All the prophecies spoke of Jesus rising from the dead on the third day; that at least must be included, and to get to that point some record of his burial must also be made. Mark does rather more than the minimum. He takes care to name eyewitnesses both to the dying and the burial. He records the actions of Joseph of Arimathaea, and that the death of Jesus is officially confirmed. The burial itself is hasty; the anointing would have to wait until Sabbath regulations permitted – but anointing is in their mind, the completion of the rituals of death, so there is no thought of resurrection, however many times Jesus had spoken of it.

One feature of these last few paragraphs is rarely commented on: there is a change in the feeling of the storytelling. All the tension has gone out of the language until the last few verses, when what is being said creates its own impact. The final words are the most astonishing way to end, but these are the last words we have from the original creators of this Gospel: *'They said nothing to anyone, for they were afraid.'* (Mark 16:8)
From the second century Christians of every generation have found this ending difficult – so uncomfortable that sometime during that century at least one other ending was attached to Mark's Gospel. Our present verses 9 to 20 are by a different hand and seem to draw on other Gospels to give this Gospel a 'proper' ending. The verdict is almost unanimous that to end a book with *'for they were afraid'* is absolutely unthinkable; to end a Gospel without the risen Lord appearing – let alone all the other remarkable things recorded in the other Gospels – seems to leave a great hole in the witness which Mark gives us. Various inventive explanations have been offered, but unhappiness remains, and the feeling that there really must be more. So strong are our expectations that readers of this Gospel have largely been left baffled by the sudden and unexpected way this Gospel comes to an end.

But this response to the way Mark's Gospel ends is fuelled entirely by our expectations and needs. Generations of Christians have been brought up on the resurrection stories of the other Gospels, especially those in John's Gospel, and we find it inconceivable that a Gospel should end in any other way. So essential is the resurrection of Jesus to our understanding of the Christian faith – and in particular the evidence of eye-witnesses who met and saw the risen Christ (for Christians of every generation have been challenged to provide their evidence for such an exceptional event) – that readers or listeners are still waiting for the final glory of the Jesus story (as they see it) when the end comes. Add to that the very natural expectations of how any book should end, and the puzzlement is complete.

So strong are these expectations that it is almost impossible to receive what Mark has given us; we expect this Gospel to conform to the patterns we are familiar with from the other Gospels with which it is placed. Each of them, in their different ways, brings their account to an orderly conclusion, and they round off what they have written in a way that tells the reader clearly that the book is complete. But this pattern belongs to the written word; what Mark has given us is different in many ways, not least because it is oral in nature. It is just not Mark's style to round things off nicely, as we would expect of any written work. The ending (Mark 16:1 to 8) needs to be treated as the rest of the Gospel is treated, rather than trying to fit it into a pattern which is alien to its nature.

The story itself contains all the clues we could possibly need to receive what we are given. As listeners, we go with the women to the graveside; the concern about moving the huge stone is understandable. Even the fact that they are going to the tomb to complete the rituals of death is not out of place – indeed it is very important because it tells us what the women are thinking: they think of Jesus as dead, and that they are going to the tomb to offer him their final tribute of love and care.

But nothing is as they expected: the stone has been rolled away; in the tomb they are met by a young man in white; the body itself is gone. Each of these facts is more than fact: we are being told that death has not been able to contain Jesus; the young man is in white to tell the women (and the audience) that this unexpected turn of events is of God; the women respond as people confronted by an act of God. Even the message they are charged with sets this moment in the context of what Jesus has already told them: he will go ahead of them to Galilee, as promised; and the final action – the women fleeing from the grave in fear and terror – is saying more than simply what the women did. The fear of the women is not different in nature from the fear we have already seen several times in this Gospel. In each case – the stilling of the storm, the healing of Legion, Jesus walking on the water – fear is the response of those who do not believe, but find themselves confronted by a power and an action which is in every way divine. It would be very odd if somehow the fear of the women who ran from the grave was any different.

The conclusion presented to us by the actions of the women is this: here is an act of divine power, God fulfilling his promises in a way they have not expected. They have yet to come to believe, whatever Jesus had said, and in turning on their heels and running they confirm that what has confronted them is not some human conundrum but the power of God at work.

What then of the ending? Mark's ending, perhaps more than any other, enables us to share the shock of the resurrection, to get inside the experience which turned the world upside down, and to allow our minds to be open to the possibility that this resurrection is very real, that it is of God, and those of us who are brought to this moment by Mark are being challenged to believe, rather than run away in confusion.

Letting the Gospel speak

St Mark's Gospel has lived in the shadow of the other Gospels since the second century when they were brought together. Ignored by the Fathers, dismissed as having rather ordinary language – not up to the literary standard of the others, with an abrupt beginning and a frankly difficult end – this Gospel has suffered from other people's conclusions about it. What this review (and it was in no way exhaustive) has told us is that this Gospel is a live, vibrant and very powerful work, created by the action of faithful Christians as they went about the task for which the Church was brought into being – telling those outside the community of believers the good news of Jesus.

In so many ways those conclusions blinded generations to the true nature of the Gospel in front of them. If this study has been properly alert to the signals this Gospel has sent us about itself, we must now think of it as an oral work, shaped by its use and designed for a particular purpose. Its drive has been to bring those who hear it to a commitment of faith, and its content reflects that. It is no wonder that there is so little about living the Christian life, when it was addressed to those who had not yet begun their life of discipleship. There would have been little point in giving teaching on prayer until faith had come which would have naturally expressed itself in prayer. This is a focused and well-directed work which was widely known and used by the Church. We know from the other Gospels just how much was not included, but the reason why none of it was included must be that it did not serve the purpose for which this Gospel came into being.

The reason why this Gospel was so little used by the Fathers in their writings and teaching of the Church is that the needs of the Church changed; the focus of almost all their writing and teaching was how to live the Christian life and what Christians should rightly believe. The other Gospels were better suited to their purposes and the challenges of their day. We have also been too easily misled by Papias whose description of Mark as being written by a follower of Peter was far too easily accepted.

If St Mark's Gospel is to come into its own, it must be used as an oral work, preferably as a whole rather than by reading snippets taken out of context, and first and foremost it needs to be used among those who are enquiring about the faith or are young in the faith. Its freshness and brevity will speak with great power because it is being used for the purpose for which it was created.

CHAPTER THREE

Matthew – The Scribe

For many people, St Matthew's Gospel should be called 'The Great Gospel.' With the Sermon on the Mount and some of the most commanding parables this Gospel seems to be the most complete of them all. It stretches from the birth of Jesus to his death and resurrection, and it ends with Christ's memorable command to his followers to *'Go, therefore to all nations and make them my disciples.'* (Matthew 28:19) If our study of the opening words showed us that Matthew deliberately set out to write scripture, its final words tell us of the scope of his vision and purpose. We are left in no doubt that he wrote in the tradition of Jewish scripture, and used many of its methods and charactcristics, but the ultimate purpose of this Gospel goes far beyond the range and intentions of the Jewish scriptures. It is clear that the writer, whoever he was, is not to be identified with Matthew, the disciple. No one would have been able to experience all that the disciples went through, and then write such a detached record. Matthew, the writcr of the Gospel, is a man steeped in the Jewish scriptures who has been able to collect and order a great variety of material, and bring it into a single whole. Some of the material (such as we find in Mark's Gospel) was oral; there may, perhaps, have been some written material – collections of parables or sayings – but Matthew has been the master of what he included and how he expressed it. What is beyond doubt is that this Gospel has fed and guided Christians of every generation since, and our debt to its author is immense.

Our study of the opening verses makes it clear that we are to expect a very different Gospel from the pen of Matthew. Suggestions that Matthew was actually writing a fuller version of Mark are simply wide of the mark. Matthew did not look to the earlier Gospel to give him guidance or provide a model; his guidance and inspiration came from elsewhere. In style as well as content the two Gospels provide stark contrasts: Mark originally was oral; Matthew is written and makes the most of the strengths of the written word. Mark is sparing on the amount of teaching he includes – even then some of the parables he included were told more for what they gave to the storyline than for purposes of teaching; Matthew includes considerable bodies of teaching, not least the 'Sermons.' Mark has a strong storyline and everything is included in the telling of the stories; Matthew sits loose to any storyline, often arranging his materials in blocks, with little continuity between the different episodes. Above all, Matthew's record is more of a report on the events of Jesus' life and ministry; he communicated with his readers in a different way from Mark. Even when the most remarkable events are recorded by Matthew, the account we are given is quite matter of fact. These differences will be highlighted as Matthew's Gospel is reviewed, and we must be prepared for the Gospels to be different in nature and purpose and scope.

Matthew himself has given us the strongest possible clue to the real inspiration for his writing. His references to the Jewish scriptures are to be found throughout the Gospel, but especially in the first few chapters. Fulfilment is his recurring theme: in Jesus the hopes of the people and the promises of God are fulfilled. For Matthew this was the real authentication of Jesus as the promised Messiah. But the driving force which impelled Matthew to take the extraordinary step of creating his magnum opus lies beyond. For him, scripture was sacred and supreme; he took profoundly seriously what it had to say and the authority it held as the 'Word of God.' He saw his record of Jesus' life and teaching as not merely adding to scripture, but completing it: he is providing its culmination. The glorious final words of this Gospel are much more than a nice way of rounding off his book: this is the full stop which completes all scripture. We are not far into his great Sermon on the Mount when we read these words: *Do not suppose that I have come to abolish the law and the prophets; I did not come to abolish but to complete.'* (Matthew 5:17) We might paraphrase his understanding of what he was undertaking in the words: 'I am not writing to reject the Jewish scriptures; I am writing to complete them.'

From birth to ministry

It is difficult to call Matthew 1:18-25 a birth story. Mary is hardly mentioned; it is the decisions and actions of Joseph which are the focus of the story. It is through him that Jesus can be said to be 'Son of David,' and gives Jesus his place in the genealogy with which the Gospel began. This is the first of many ways in which Matthew uses the traditions and practices of the Jewish scriptures. So too his use of angels and dreams is a traditional and figurative way of expressing an understanding of what God was asking Joseph and Mary to undertake. The full significance of the birth is expounded in chapter 2: *'Where is the new-born king of the Jews?'* (Matthew 2:2) The scriptures and the stars (and those who interpret them) bring an unmistakable message for king, priest and people alike; no wonder the Magi caused a stir. For the Jewish people, they could only be looking for one king, the king promised by God. Matthew sets it out in this way so that those who read what he is writing will understand the full significance of the birth he has recorded. Born in obscurity, Jesus has none of the trappings of royalty and power, in contrast to Herod who lived in a palace and found this talk of another king something of a threat. He did what any tyrant would do, and brought great pain and sorrow to innocent lives. But the king he could not kill will soon enough be bringing healing and wholeness to those in need, and will speak of his kingdom which will be different in every way from Herod's. References to the 'Kingdom of Heaven' (it might be translated 'Kingdom of the Heavens') will be found throughout the Gospel; this too is part of God's promise to his people and finds its fulfilment in the mission and ministry of Christ.

Matthew alone tells of the visit of the Magi, the flight to Egypt and the eventual return to Nazareth, evocative stories all of them, and told to reinforce what Matthew wants to convey. The gifts of the Magi are as mysterious as their givers. Where they came from and who they were is not clear; Magi could be associated with a Persian priestly caste, but it is just as likely that Matthew has chosen the title deliberately to discourage us from being too factual about our interpretation of the story. He wants us to see Christ acknowledged and worshipped as the great King of the Jews by those throughout the world who could understand the signs given by God. The star also is part of this picture; we will be in danger of missing the significance of the star if we expend too much energy in trying to identify it.

The flight to Egypt, the massacre in Bethlehem and the eventual settling of the family in Nazareth are all stories which lead up to quotations from the Old Testament. Taken together, Matthew is building up a message for his readers which has far more significance than the details of the events he records: the hand of God is to be seen at every point, even in adversity; these seemingly unconnected events fulfil the words of God spoken many centuries before.

The short chapter 3 is Matthew's account of the baptism of Jesus. We are familiar with a considerable number of details which we have already seen in St Mark's Gospel, and yet the account Matthew gives us is in many ways quite different. John's message, *'Repent, for the kingdom of Heaven is upon you'* (Matthew 3:2) is exactly the same as the message Jesus will give (Matthew 4:17). John's tone is very much of judgement, and he is particularly scathing about the Pharisees and Sadducees (not for the last time) *'Who warned you to escape from the wrath that is to come?'* (Matthew 3:7) Perhaps it is no surprise that the Gospel which sets most store by teaching the way to live the good life should be most severe on those adjudged to have fallen short. So vigorous is his language that Jesus' arrival is almost swamped by comparison.

He has also given himself a dilemma: how can Jesus come for baptism? It cannot be a mark of repentance. Obedience is the solution, and Jesus offers himself as the Son doing the Father's will. As in Mark, the descent of the Spirit and the voice from heaven follow the baptism – but the voice is not addressed to Jesus (in the second person – 'you'): Matthew makes it a proclamation for everyone to hear – not least the readers of this Gospel.

The final piece of preparation before his public ministry can begin is his trial of strength with the 'tempter.' It is a great deal fuller than the account we have in Mark, but then Matthew's introduction of Jesus has been so much more extensive, and while Mark works up to the discovery of Jesus as Son of God, Matthew wastes no time in taking up the title given to Jesus at his baptism. 'Son of God' appears twice in Matthew's account of the Temptations, and on each occasion is offered by the tempter as the reason for taking the action suggested ('Do it because you can!'). To all three suggestions from the tempter Jesus gives an answer from scripture; it is only fitting for the Son of God to be guided by God's Word in coming to understand how he will live out his obedience to the Father in the campaign to come. But this is not simple storytelling; quotations and allusions to the Old Testament almost fall over each other in this account of the Temptations, and Matthew expects his readers to pick up all the clues from their knowledge of the scriptures.

The Ministry begins

The Ministry begins, but not without Matthew grounding it in yet another text (or two) from scripture. We are not to forget the roots from which the whole story springs. As already mentioned, Jesus' call is couched in precisely the same words as John the Baptist's message – very different from Mark who implies that the need for change is not so much sin and failure, but the opportunity to be part of the promised kingdom which is very near (Mark 1:15). Suddenly, everything is changed. The language has a different feel to it, and Jesus is walking by the Sea of Galilee. The opening proclamations have been completed and Matthew takes up the story of Jesus' mission following the pattern we are familiar with from Mark. The people for whom he is writing will almost certainly know how the story of Jesus' ministry begins from the oral material circulating within the life of the Church. But Matthew does not slavishly follow Mark; we notice the absence of 'and immediately' – he has his own version of that. The first disciples are called, but there is no feeling of impetus building. While Mark takes up the story with individual actions and events, Matthew gives us a general picture. His description is extensive, both in the illnesses and diseases which Jesus encounters, and the regions from which people come. Jesus is having an enormous impact. Yet however impressive this beginning, the picture Matthew gives is little more than a prelude to the great Sermon he is about to introduce.

The Sermon on the Mount

We might be surprised that Matthew launches into the great centrepiece of his teaching so early in his Gospel, but this is an indication of the great importance he attaches to it. It stands as a foundation to all the other teaching he is planning to include in his great masterpiece. The shape of it is instructive. First he lays down the primary virtues of the spiritual life; those who live by them are *'blessed'* and are heirs to God's most generous bounty. Further, he designates those who live by this standard as the *'salt of the earth,' 'light for all the world.'* Then he lays out where he sees this work in relation to the scriptures that already exist: *'I did not come to abolish, but to complete.'* (Matthew 5:17) He expands this with a series of contrasts between the old and the new. These show that Jesus does not reject the old Commandments; he goes further than they do, seeing to the heart of every action, and speaking on a spiritual level, not so much in terms of public action. The contrast between outward action and the inward, spiritual motivation is continued into the practice of fasting, worship and prayer. This leads on to a fundamental perception of the life of faith – living under God's providence and following his ways. Finally, Matthew provides wisdom and guidance for the disciple along the way. The flow of the Sermon disguises just how careful he has been in setting out the teaching he has in mind. What we are about to hear is not an inconsequential pronouncement with little shape or purpose about it: it is an ordered and considered presentation of the teaching Matthew most wants his readers to hear and live by.

The much-loved picture of Jesus going up a hill, sitting down, and beginning to speak to his disciples is disarmingly simple. It is, in fact, a piece of very careful stage-management, as full of symbolism as it is of straightforward description. And if the setting is stage-managed, so is the Sermon that follows. That should not surprise us. Matthew, the Scribe, has assembled his material and put it into the most potent form at his disposal. Far more important to him than telling the story of an event as it happened is investing the teaching of Jesus with the greatest possible authority. He therefore presents Jesus' teaching in a form that will do this, and in doing so evokes other great moments recorded in scripture, in particular the giving of the Ten Commandments in Exodus 20. So, the going up the hill recalls Moses on Mount Sinai, and the Beatitudes (as we have come to call them) make an unspoken reference back to the great Commandments of God which were the foundation of the people's life and their relationship with the living God. To the listening disciples – and to everyone who reads this passage – Matthew is presenting what he considers to be the essence of living faithfully with God, a way of life which will bring rich rewards to those who follow it. He calls them 'blessed,' a word with many layers of meaning. They are not only 'happy' – the usual meaning of the word; they are those who achieve the full life, the godly life which will be enriched by all the blessings God generously bestows. Jesus holds out to those who commit themselves to following him something deeper than moral rectitude; this is the way to the complete life, full humanity, which finds its realisation in the joy of heaven.

To begin his Sermon in this dramatic way catches the attention, but in naming *'the poor in spirit . . . the sorrowful . . . the gentle . . . those who hunger and thirst to see right prevail,'* he is also proclaiming the breadth of his appeal – not only to the religious and those who keep the law, but to precisely those people who carry the burdens of life, and those who all too often are excluded by many a religious orthodoxy. By placing them at the head of those people who will inherit God's blessings, he is giving hope to so many who feel themselves excluded. This Sermon is for everyone, just as Matthew intends the scope of his Gospel to go far beyond the scope of other scriptures.

There are two features of Jesus' teaching in general which we will see throughout this Gospel, not just in this Sermon. Time and again he makes a point of the unexpected, and such is the vividness of each picture that there is no mistaking his meaning. The Beatitudes are no exception. The first surprise is those who are selected for consolation and blessing. Whatever translation we use, it is a most arresting selection – many of them are usually considered the 'have-nots of our world' and the boon they are promised is equally surprising: *'the kingdom of heaven is theirs'* (Matthew 5:10). What Christ offers is staggeringly generous – life in all its fullness for those whom life has taught not to hope for anything.

The next three Beatitudes – *'those who show mercy . . . those whose hearts are pure . . . the peacemakers'* are rather more orthodox; the boon expressed by Jesus might even be said to be the expected outcome of such virtue. Each of them deserves its place in the spiritual life of any disciple and in the hierarchy of qualities that are desirable. Matthew sets out these foundations for discipleship, but inevitably there is a price to be paid for putting the teaching in this form. *'Blessed are . . . '* sounds very different from *'Thou shalt . . .' Thou shalt not . . .'* What Matthew writes is a proclamation, not a command, but when put in this form the difference becomes less clear. Matthew is intending to say 'This is the way to live,' and when this is understood the difference between *'Blessed are'* and *'Thou shalt'* is a great deal smaller.

There is, however, one consideration which may well shed some light on how these Beatitudes come to be in the form in which Matthew records them. Jesus' teaching in all the Gospels has great clarity; he uses striking pictures and images to convey his message. Yet preachers of every generation have struggled to give convincing meaning to the phrase *'poor in spirit.'* It has no direct Old Testament counterpart, and although 'the poor' or 'the poor man' is not infrequently an upright and faithful person who is unjustly suffering, the scriptures give no guidance when we come to this phrase. The phrase *'to see right prevail'* is equally unconvincing, and changes the meaning of what Jesus is saying altogether. It may well be that Matthew has added these phrases because they fit in with his great scheme. The fact that Luke, who only records the first four Beatitudes, omits these phrases suggests that the wording we have in chapter 5 reflects Matthew's own original approach. Matthew is doing more than simply recording a number of sayings of Jesus; he is shaping them as well, and this will prepare us for a major theme which develops later in the chapter.

The final Beatitude, *'Blessed are you who are persecuted in the cause of right'* (Matthew 5:10) brings a change. Jesus addresses directly his disciples and those who suffer for following him, and he continues to address them throughout the rest of the Sermon. For them the road will be hard, but they stand in an honoured tradition – the prophets too were persecuted. But it will not be hardship which will define them; they are to be *'salt to the world'* and *'light for all the world.'* They are to stand out in the world around them and make a difference wherever they are to be found. They are not to hide away as if discipleship was a private matter; their lives are to bring light (hope, goodness, a new way of living) to those with whom they come into contact.

But before Matthew is able to develop the theme which has begun to appear, he is careful to set one thing on record: *'Do not suppose that I have come to abolish the law and the prophets; I did not come to abolish but to complete.'* (Matthew 5:17) Matthew would have been horrified if what he had written had been interpreted as rejecting God's law. For him, the law still stands – but there is a difference: those who are being hailed as 'blessed' all display inner qualities rather than external actions. This is a distinction which the Sermon develops. There is a series of contrasts: *'You have heard that our forefathers were told . . . But what I tell you is this . . .'* (Matthew 5:21, 27, 33, 38, 43.) What we notice is that there is a fundamental difference between the Commandments of Exodus

20 and the Beatitudes. While the law in many ways is public and describes actions – essential if the law is to be the foundation of national life – Jesus' teaching is individual, personal and spiritual. While the law speaks of murder, Jesus teaches about anger and contempt; the law speaks of adultery, but Jesus teaches about lust and temptation; the law speaks of *'taking the name of the Lord in vain;'* Jesus calls us not to indulge in invocations of any kind. The contrast is between the command which governs the external action, and Jesus' teaching which sees to the inner working of the heart. But this is not simply a long list of directions as to how to behave: it is leading up to the real foundation to all good living which is to be found in the ways and will of God. He·is to be our standard, since he is our Creator and the author of the life we live. From this foundation spring very different responses to the challenges life brings. In place of 'an eye for an eye' there is generosity not retaliation, reconciliation not animosity; in place of 'love your neighbour and hate your enemy' (the old standard) Jesus' followers are to *'Love your enemies and pray for your persecutors'* (Matthew 5:44); this is the way God treats us.

The contrast between outward show and inner reality continues in chapter 6, not least in what might be called the religious sphere of alms-giving, fasting and prayer. But Matthew adds another dimension: the inward spiritual life, even when it is hidden, is met by God's open blessing. For Matthew, virtue and goodness have their reward – a very Jewish understanding, which is reflected strongly in this part of the Sermon especially. Whatever is done, be it prayer or alms-giving or even fasting, must above all have the hidden quality of being from the heart; for nothing is hidden to God. But there is much more than 'don't make a show of it' about Jesus' teaching. The practices he describes were commonplace in Jesus' day; his practical direction *'go into a room by yourself, shut the door, and pray to your Father who is in secret'* (Matthew 6:6) has been a guide for anyone exploring the world of prayer since. So too his *'do not go babbling on like the heathen'* brings a focus to prayer which centres its attention on God, his presence and his readiness to respond in generosity and love.

The crown of his teaching on prayer is the Lord's Prayer itself (Matthew 6:9-13). This prayer has been at the heart of Christian spirituality and devotion from the very beginning, but by the time Matthew commits it to paper it may well have already become rounded and formalised by use both publicly and privately. Matthew's version of the Lord's Prayer has a number of features which have parallels in Jewish prayers of the day, but these do not take away from the uniqueness and clarity of the prayer we are given. Those who use the prayer regularly are helped by being given words with which to approach God. It establishes our relationship with him, so that we pray it as children of our great and heavenly Father (given us by the One we acknowledge as the Son); it gives us words so that we can fulfil our role as children, while turning to God for those things which can only come from him. It ends with the very Jewish paean of praise which should never be absent from prayer to the great and glorious God. The long ending of the prayer is not in all manuscripts, but very soon became an indispensable part of it (although Luke, who gives us a much shorter Lord's Prayer, does not include it).

The life of faith is also a life lived under the providence of God. Preoccupation with material things, even good things, divides the commitment of the disciple to his Lord. Faith means allowing God to be God and Lord even of the necessities of daily living. Much of chapter 7 is an extension of this theme, and is greatly reminiscent of the Jewish Wisdom literature which Matthew will have known. Many of the sayings of Jesus in this passage have little natural connection with each other, but all contribute their own teaching or piece of wisdom. Each begins with a statement which is followed by an insight that answers the first statement; each is perceptive and neat, but when taken together they create a body of material which provides a ready guide for the disciple. Such is the striking nature of some of these sayings that phrases from them have entered our daily use of language ('pearls before swine', 'wolf in sheep's clothing'). Many of the sayings might not be thought to be specifically Christian, but they speak of an attitude to life which is clear and distinctive. Little wonder that over the centuries this Sermon has been regarded as the pinnacle of Christ's teaching – as Matthew intended it to be.

The parable with which the Sermon ends is fresh, colourful and pointed. The teaching which has been given is to be acted upon, and is intended to shape lives and guide discipleship. Jesus speaks with authority, and as the story of the healing of the centurion's servant emphasises (Matthew 8:5-13), authority is to be met by obedience. This is the mental framework of the whole Gospel, and underscores the unique contribution Matthew has made to the life of the Church. He has given to the Christian Community a scripture which provides for the life of the disciple what the Law did for the Jewish people.

The Wider Ministry

The Jewish scriptures were not just books of law with the necessary regulations for community use. As the People of God, they also had a history that bound them together and gave them both an identity and a shared faith. It is this which has set them apart throughout their life as a people. Matthew also needs to provide this for the Christian community. Christians needed to know who they were, and to have a clear understanding of how they were distinct both from the Jews and also from other faiths in the world around them. Above all, they needed to be given a narrative that would equip them with an inner self-confidence which would enable them to live the life of faith. The narrative that makes this possible is centred on Jesus. His actions, as well as his teachings, must be part of that narrative; miracles of healing and feeding will be part of the storyline, as well as encounters and conflicts which serve to illustrate his closeness to God.

Matthew tends to organise his material in blocks; so, following the Sermon on the Mount, he sets out a series of healing miracles (Matthew 8:1 to 9:38) and this, in turn, is followed by another Sermon – on Mission (Matthew 10:14 to end). Many of the miracle stories Matthew records are already familiar to us from our study of Mark, but a number of features of this material should not escape us. In no way has Matthew felt obliged to follow Mark, either in the order in which the stories are told, or in the way the events are recorded. In his account of the healing of the leper Matthew shortens the story given us in Mark (Mark 1:40-45); details of Mark's account are omitted, especially the actions of the man in making known what Jesus had done which resulted in Jesus having to stay in the open country. Equally, Matthew's account of the healing of Peter's (Mark still calls him Simon) mother-in-law is shortened and changed, and the healing of the sick at evening (Matthew 8:16 and 17) is a mere shadow of the story told in Mark, with none of the drama of people waiting until the Sabbath regulations no longer applied before they brought their sick to Jesus. Matthew does, however, end the story with a quotation from Isaiah. The contrast between the two ways of telling the stories is instructive. Matthew reports what Jesus did, but he excludes everything which might take the reader's attention away from Jesus. It is not the power of the experience of Jesus healing which carries his message, but the quotation from Isaiah which provides authentication. While Mark builds a storyline with one story preparing the way for the next, Matthew's account is flat – a series of unconnected events presented as evidence that God's purpose is being fulfilled. We are also shown by Matthew's careful (but ruthless) filleting of the stories he has received that he is in no way inhibited in his handling of the material. One can only assume that he has exercised the same freedom when handling other material of which we have no knowledge. In truth, Matthew is not a great storyteller, and his filleting of the stories he uses sometimes destroys the inner logic of the story he is telling. His focus is elsewhere. Some of the great parables at the end of the Gospel, however, seem to be treated differently, and these we shall examine when the time comes.

So chapters 8 and 9, mostly a collection of miracles, give us another part of our heritage. Jesus is the healer, even of leprosy – sometimes talked of as 'living death.' Though others deeply fear it, Jesus is master over it. Such authority is recognised by the centurion who came to him; in turn Jesus recognises his faith. Matthew does not let us move on until the implications of this Gentile's faith have been underlined. Heaven is for everyone, which may come as a shock to those who assume that simply being born a member of God's Chosen People was enough to guarantee them a place. Faith and discipleship are the way to enter the promised kingdom; for some it will mean a change of life, and breaking ties which otherwise will stifle their response.

Throughout these two chapters the great variety of miracles or encounters are so told that words of Jesus complete them, or people reflect on what Jesus has done. Some remarkable moments are given us as part of our heritage – among them the stilling of the storm and the raising of the young daughter of an official. Matthew does not dwell long on any of them; together they present us with a picture of Jesus that is powerful, compassionate and authoritative. Jesus is a man of action as well as words; he must be followed not with lip service but with dedication. These stories of healing (with a few challenging sayings also included) come to an end with a very general picture of Jesus' ministry. But Matthew is already looking forward to what follows. It is Jesus' pity and compassion which moved him both to heal and preach to the people; in time this will also be the driving force for the Church's mission and it is to this that Matthew now turns.

A Sermon on Mission

Up to this point the disciples have been little more than companions and spectators of Jesus' mission. Now they are to be directly involved, and so Matthew names them. He is not relating their call to discipleship, simply recording their names. Even so, there are some differences from the other Gospels in the names we are given and the way it is expressed. But although they stand ready to receive their marching orders, there is more than a hint that the orders given in this passage are not so much for the disciples as members of the Church carrying out missionary work in Matthew's day. Most puzzling of all is the instruction to avoid certain places and to direct their message to *'the lost sheep of the house of Israel'* (Matthew 10:6). Nowhere else in the Gospels (not even in Matthew) is such a limitation put on the mission Jesus is engaged in, although one suggestion is that this is a strategic direction being given to the people for whom Matthew is writing. He expects this phrase to have specific meaning for those who hear it; it may well reflect the way a predominantly Jewish Church might talk about their fellow Jews who do not yet believe. By the same token, the choice of lodging is hardly likely to have been much of a concern to an itinerant preacher. Opposition and even rejection is to be expected, and the disciples are given clear direction as to how to deal with it.

As with the Sermon on the Mount, Matthew has collected material on the subject of mission from different sources. We recognise material from Mark 4, Mark 6 and Mark 13 (and possibly Mark 9), and by bringing it all together in this way readers are given an intense passage, moving from one subject to another without a pause. For the most part, Jesus' instruction lays the foundations for anyone living and bearing witness in a hostile world. They are directions for the long-term, not a brief campaign of limited duration, such as the storyline suggests. This is a reminder that Matthew has not lost sight of the people for whom he is writing, and their needs in a world that all too readily rejects what they stand for.

The general note of Jesus leaving that place and taking his mission to neighbouring towns (Matthew 11:1) is a way of marking the end of the Sermon on Mission and providing a setting for the next body of material. Strangely, he makes no mention of the disciples going out – or of returning to Jesus. The purpose of mission is to bring people to faith, but in reality all kinds of responses are made, from faith to doubt and disbelief. In this setting it is no less a person than John the Baptist who puts into words what everyone is asking: *'Are you the one who is to come?'* (Matthew 11:3) The reply is a ringing proclamation of what Jesus is doing, all the more emphatic because it is demonstrating how God's promises through the prophet Isaiah (Isaiah 35) are being fulfilled in action. John the Baptist too has played his part in confirming who Jesus is since he is the promised Elijah (Matthew 11:14) and the messenger whose task it is to *'clear a path'* ahead of God's promised One (Malachi 3:1). Those who know the scriptures have all the evidence they need to recognise Jesus; how terrible, then, that it is especially those who are best equipped to understand what they are seeing and hearing who fail to come to faith. Jesus chides the experts – and the places where he healed the sick and raised the dead. It is the ordinary folk who are receptive and believe. It is they whom Jesus invites and welcomes; they shall know the fulfilment and the wholeness which are marks of the promised kingdom.

The controversies of chapter 12 need little introduction; many of the stories are featured in St Mark's Gospel, but in each case Matthew has put his mark on what he records by expanding the arguments and adding further sayings which have much the same combative nature. In the middle of it all, Matthew introduces the great Servant Song from Isaiah 42, a complete contrast to everything he records around it, but a reminder of who Jesus is, as his actions confirm. Controversy cannot have been absent from Jesus' ministry, and it was not absent from the life of the Church. Matthew provides material which will equip the Church of his day to answer the criticisms it is bound to face. As the chapter goes on, it becomes increasingly clear that the fundamental argument runs something like this: 'In word and deed, Jesus has fulfilled all the prophecies, all the promises of God; despite everything, you have failed to recognise him.' Matthew takes great care to show how unreasonable their rejection of Jesus is. Three times in the chapter we hear (in slightly different forms) 'and something greater is here' – greater than the Temple, the focus of God's presence with his people (Matthew 12:6); greater than Jonah, who called the people of Nineveh to repent (Matthew 12:41); greater than Solomon, whose wisdom dazzled the Queen of Sheba (Matthew 12:42). Jesus not only fulfils scripture, he outshines those who have gone before him in all he is and does. The final event in this passage is a visit from his mother and brothers. So different is Matthew's presentation of these controversies that Mark's storyline has been left well behind. Now, however, Matthew returns to it. His readers will already be familiar with the story of the visit of Jesus' mother and brothers, and the words of Jesus: *'Whoever does the will of my heavenly Father is my brother and sister and mother.'*

Mark's order of things brings Jesus back to the Sea of Galilee and an opportunity to teach the people. Matthew follows this order, telling the parable of the sower and Jesus' explanation of it in his own way. But he cannot tell the story without putting his own mark on it and making small adjustments throughout. Whether Mark's rather more simple language grated on him we shall never know, but the changes he makes – even when telling substantially the same story – do not seem to have any significant reason behind them. What, for instance, is the reason for reversing the numbers at the climax of the story? (Mark works up to a hundred; Matthew begins with one hundred, then sixty, then thirty.) There does not seem to be any deliberate rewriting of Mark's wording; the real explanation may be that this is bound to happen when material, which originally was spoken, is committed to the page; as Matthew is further from the event and the impact of the moment, he naturally tells the parable to inform rather than engage, and this change of purpose enables him (as he would wish) to include further material not present in the earlier account.

In particular, Matthew is keen to include material which speaks of the kingdom of Heaven. Seven short parables or sayings under this heading follow Jesus' explanation of the parable of the sower – each of them little more than a snapshot, but together they make a collage which speaks of the richness of this ultimate blessing that Jesus promises. It is of such value that any amount of sacrifice would be worth making in order to be able to enter the promised kingdom. Matthew formally ends this body of teaching – but we are told something more: his emphasis is on 'understanding' – not just hearing the words but being able to put them into practice. His reference to 'old' and 'new' reminds us that Matthew includes both the Jewish scriptures and his new scripture as essential for being able to live the life which will bring the believer to the promised kingdom.

Matthew has already told the story of the stilling of the storm, the healing of Legion (Mark 4:35 to 5:20) and the raising of Jairus' daughter (Mark 5:21-43); he included them in the body of material in chapters 8 and 9 in which he recorded a number of Jesus' miracles. He now takes up the familiar storyline with Jesus' visit to his home-town. It can only have been a most painful visit. The people he had grown up with could not see him as anything more than one of them. That he had great wisdom and miraculous powers was beyond dispute, but they could not see beyond their human knowledge of him to understand the true significance of what they had seen and heard. No more could Herod, whose superstitious explanation of what Jesus was doing was prompted more by guilt than insight.

Matthew includes his own version of the sad story of John the Baptist's death. Though recognisably the same event as we find in St Mark's Gospel, the story is much changed – and not very convincingly so: in Mark, it was Herodias who hated John and wanted to kill him. Herod went in awe of John, knowing him to be a good and holy man (Mark 6:20). Herod's distress at the dilemma he found himself in is only credible if Herod honoured and respected John. It is important that the death of John the Baptist is recorded somewhere in the Gospel; Matthew chooses to do it at this point, though he seems to have no enthusiasm for the task. It does, however, give Jesus a reason for withdrawing, if only temporarily, from his public ministry, and so the circumstances which led to the feeding of the five thousand are created.

The traditional order of events brings Matthew to the feeding and the episode of Jesus coming to the disciples walking on the water. This is part of the 'Christian story' and Matthew sets out these dramatic events in his own way. These stories have a different role in this Gospel from the part they played in St Mark's Gospel; here they are told to fill out the story of Jesus which every Christian needs to know. For the most part, changes from the earlier account are small and insignificant, but Matthew makes his own addition. He tells of Peter getting out of the boat and walking towards Jesus – and beginning to sink. Peter's failure contrasts dramatically with what Jesus has done, and the response of amazement and worship expresses what must, in his mind, be the appropriate response after such an astonishing experience.

The general pattern of ministry is taken up again, but experts from Jerusalem are waiting to challenge Jesus on his attitude towards the revered 'tradition of the Fathers' which for religious people was sacrosanct. Jesus' response is pointed and unapologetic – and clearly caused a stir. Matthew records this verbal skirmish in such a way that a quotation from Isaiah has the last word, and Jesus elaborates both to the crowd and the disciples on the real significance of the stand he has taken. Matthew, the Scribe, does not miss the opportunity to re-arrange the list of sins to conform to the order of the Commandments.

Details of the encounter with a Canaanite woman are also considerably changed, suggesting that Matthew's understanding of the event was a great deal more literal than was Mark's. There we find spontaneous interplay between Jesus and the woman ('children' and 'dogs' being common shorthand for the way Jews used to talk about Jews and Gentiles). This whole dimension is missing in Matthew, which makes Jesus' response all the more out of character. Nevertheless, the healing happens and introduces a general description of the work Jesus did in this predominantly Gentile area.

The traditional pattern re-asserts itself with the feeding of the four thousand, the clash with the Pharisees (and Matthew adds the Sadducees), and the tortuous explanation of a difficult saying as they crossed the sea. It is always a bad sign when explanations have to follow a parable: explanations are only employed when there is no understanding – and it is not at all certain that even Matthew really understands what Jesus is driving at. His explanation that the disciples must avoid 'the teaching of the Pharisees and Sadducees' (Matthew 16:12) is far from convincing.

Missing from this sequence of events is the gradual healing of a blind man. In Mark, it served as a symbolic prelude to Peter's acknowledgement of Jesus as the 'Messiah,' which takes place at Caesarea Philippi. Matthew sees no need for such preparation and plunges into one of the key moments of the Gospel. Yet it is all told in such a matter of fact way that it is difficult for the reader to appreciate just what a momentous occasion it is. Even Jesus' summons to the disciples could be mistaken for just another piece of teaching. Yet Matthew does have his own perspective on this pivotal moment. Jesus' response to Peter when he acknowledges him to be the Christ is fulsome. His recognition has come from God, and is not the product of human reasoning or deduction. Divine inspiration has revealed a truth that no one could have guessed at – indeed it seems that despite everything Jesus had said and done, no one had. But the blessing of Christ also carries with it a further duty: Peter has shown himself to be equipped to shoulder further responsibilities: he is to be the 'rock' on which the Church will be built.

Almost nowhere else is there a direct reference to the Church (although it was for the Church that Matthew was writing). We are given no encouragement, except in this reference, to come to any conclusion about what Jesus envisaged in the future. That there will be a future is certain – because the future belongs to God, and it will be in that future that the fulfilment of all God's promises will be realised. For Matthew the Church has a vital part to play: it was through the Church that he saw the fulfilment of God's plans; it was within the Church that Christ would be believed in and followed; it was for the Church that Matthew was writing. This is the insight which lights up this pivotal moment.

The Journey to Jerusalem

The journey to Jerusalem where Jesus will live out his destiny stands behind the next four chapters, but before the journey can begin we are to glimpse Christ's glory. This moment stands at the beginning of the journey much as the Baptism takes place before Jesus' public ministry begins. As Matthew tells it, the story of the Transfiguration is a mixture of symbol, scriptural reference and description: Jesus' face shines much as Moses' face shone after communing with God; the voice prompts a response much as the Children of Israel responded to the voice at Sinai; the cloud is a symbol of God's presence, and all this took place on a mountain-top – the place of meeting with God. It is a moment of revelation and transition, so that we are left in no doubt that the Christ who now makes his way to Jerusalem has the unique glory of the Son of God.

For the last chapter or so Matthew has followed the pattern of events which may well have become accepted before he began his Gospel. So, as in St Mark's Gospel, Jesus confirms that John the Baptist is the promised Elijah, and he heals a boy that the disciples were unable to heal. As they make their way through Galilee, Jesus tells the disciples once again that *'The Son of Man is to be handed over into the power of men, and they will kill him'* (Matthew 17:22). Into this expected pattern of events he introduces a story about Temple tax. For all Jesus' radical teaching, he remains within the Jewish community and shares its burdens.

In chapter 18 Jesus is again teaching the disciples. The kingdom of heaven is his theme – the phrase occurs three times in a very few verses – and he draws in additional material to fill out the theme. In fact, good teacher that he is, he brings order to an intense and confusing passage in Mark, and sets out sides of discipleship he has not yet been able to write about. Clearly he has the life of the Christian community very much in mind – responsibility for one another – what to do if things go wrong – how the disciple needs to be single-minded about following Christ. Finally, he draws together the different threads in a major parable – ending it with the pointed comment: *'That is how my heavenly Father will deal with you, unless you each forgive your brother from your hearts'* (Matthew 18:35). It is one of the parables only to be found in Matthew, and it may well be that he is drawing on a written source which contained a number of such parables. It has all the hallmarks of Jesus' clarity and originality. Its range goes far beyond the editorial comment with which Matthew ends this section, and the perceptive portrayal of the king in the story says a great deal more about God's compassion and readiness to forgive than could easily be expressed in any other way.

Chapter 19 begins with a reference to the progress of the journey, and Matthew very much follows the traditional order by taking up the question of marriage discipline. He re-orders his account of the event, as we have come to expect, and adds further material which reflects questions that may well have been current in the Church when he was writing.

The approach of a stranger brings a change of subject. The man asks, *'Teacher, what good must I do to gain eternal life?'* (Matthew 19:16) The question was about eternal life, but it is his present situation that Jesus addresses. He is the slave of his wealth, so that when Jesus suggests giving it away in order to be free to follow him, the young man left, quite unable to take up Jesus' invitation. It is a situation not confined to this one stranger, and Jesus takes up the subject, not least with the well-known saying, *'it is easier for a camel to pass through the eye of a needle than for a rich man to enter the kingdom of God.'* (It was a saying that had already become set in that particular form of words; Matthew would not have willingly used the phrase 'kingdom of God' if that form of words had not already become established.) Even so, the mention of 'kingdom' suggests to Matthew (always so keen that faithfulness shall be rewarded) that a far greater reward is prepared for those who suffer privation for the sake of the faith. The sentence with which Mark ends his similar passage is quoted verbatim – *'many who are first will be last, and the last first'* and Matthew caps the episode (as he often does with a passage of teaching) with a major parable on the theme of those words.

The parable of the landowner and the labourers is one of Matthew's more extensive parables, and almost certainly also belongs to the same written source as the parable at the end of chapter 18. The story is told in full; there has been no filleting which we have seen elsewhere, and we are allowed to follow the logic of the story from beginning to end. But although Matthew prefers direct teaching to symbolism in the way he uses his material, not even he can avoid the indirect reference to Israel and the promised kingdom in the story about the vineyard's owner.

The road to Jerusalem is nearing its end, but before the final approach Matthew records the fullest prophecy Jesus makes about his own destiny, and, as in Mark, this is followed by an ambitious request. Matthew softens the inappropriate nature of the request by saying that it was made by the mother of the two sons of Zebedee. Jesus' response is as clear and unequivocal as the request is inappropriate: Jesus has come to serve, not rule; he is to give himself so that others shall be saved. There is no place for ambition in discipleship – how very different from the world around.

The final act before Jesus enters Jerusalem is the healing of two blind men – one wonders whether Matthew simply got confused; perhaps the way Bartimaeus is named in St Mark's Gospel suggested to him that there must have been two. Matthew, however, does not follow the earlier Gospel in speaking of the blind men 'following Jesus in the way,' a phrase which suggests discipleship.

The Jerusalem Ministry

Matthew's account of Jesus' entry into Jerusalem (Matthew 21:1-11) and his action in clearing the Temple of its commercial trappings (Matthew 21:12 and 13) make a dramatic sequence – far more coherent as a whole than the account of the events in St Mark's Gospel. Scripture is used at every point to authenticate Jesus' action, and the words and actions of the crowd make it clear that they are welcoming a king – their king – the Son of David, no less, which must have created a stir. Matthew's reading of Zechariah may have prompted him to talk of two animals instead of the one beast of burden of which the prophet talked. Jesus' prophetic action could not have been mistaken by the authorities: it was an open challenge to recognise him, as well as an act of sharp criticism of the practices which had taken root in the Temple. He puts the Temple to another use, one of healing and restoring sight – the very things for which the Temple should have stood. By changing the sequence of events, however, Matthew had lost sight of the reason in the earlier Gospel, for wrapping the story of the cursing of the fig-tree around the re-ordering of the Temple. He is, however, bound to include it as it had become an accepted part of the Jerusalem ministry.

Jesus is challenged about his actions, but he moves the debate on with a question of his own. For the chief priests' and elders' authority is something that is received: the implication of Jesus' question is that his authority comes from God, and has not been bestowed upon him by some human means, however religious. But Matthew is quite unable to resist including another parable before resuming the expected order of things: the parable of the two sons (Matthew 21:28-31) and the meaning given it by Jesus ensures that the rift between Jesus and the authorities is getting wider, and after the parable of the owner of the vineyard and the evil tenants (Matthew 21:33-43) it becomes a chasm. A third parable completes this part of Jesus' confrontation of the authorities. The parable of the wedding feast (Matthew 22:1-14) builds on the momentum of the first two parables, and like the story about a vineyard has something of a theological subtext. Traditionally, heaven was spoken of as being like a wedding feast, so Jesus does not have to explain that those who do not recognise Jesus and believe in him will exclude themselves from the promised kingdom to come. Twenty-first century minds often find the action of the king in the parable unnecessarily harsh; for Jesus and people of his day this was the dramatic colour they would have expected.

In turn both the Pharisees and the Sadducees put Jesus to the test, but are shown up for their pains. Each hoped to trap Jesus, but neither could match the breadth or depth of his vision. Paying tribute to Caesar had become an issue in some religious quarters; paying tribute was thought akin to apostasy by some. Jesus has no trouble with what is legal and honest, so long as worship and devotion are centred on God. In the same way, Jesus refuses to be pushed into a corner by the selective use of the scriptures; he uses scripture to make his case and to show how far his critics fall short of understanding the very things they trusted in to guide them. In the end, the combined forces of both parties cannot touch the natural authority Jesus has both as teacher and interpreter of scripture. His answer completes the duel he has had with the leading groups and authorities among the Jewish people. Each had challenged him on their own terms, but none had been able to match his wisdom and understanding.

Finally, Jesus puts his questions to them. Inevitably these are about their understanding of the Messiah, but his questions are answered with silence. Those who came to him have been found wanting, and Jesus' judgement on them is utterly damning, and a series of criticisms denouncing them follows: 'Alas for you, scribes and Pharisees' Jesus says six times, and roundly condemns them for their sin and failure. He rounds off his extended condemnation with the heartfelt lament:

> 'O Jerusalem, Jerusalem, the city that murders the prophets and stones the messengers sent to her! How often have I longed to gather your children, as a hen gathers her brood under her wings; but you would not let me! Look! There is your temple, forsaken by God and laid waste. I tell you, you will not see me until the time when you say: 'Blessed is he who comes in the name of the Lord!'

Matthew now turns to the 'end of time' teaching which we also saw in Mark 13. He follows quite closely what we heard in Mark, omitting some verses he has already used and adding a few details that bring colour to the passage. This is an important element in the Gospel for the Christian community, which has had to face considerable opposition and persecution even before Matthew wrote. It is essential that the faithful know that their difficulties are not unexpected, that God is still in charge and that the final outcome of their faith is the promised kingdom. He makes specific reference to the Book of Daniel which in its day spoke to the suffering faithful, and Matthew sees himself giving much the same message to the Church of his day. He does, however add three great parables whose length and fullness suggest the importance given to them. The parable of the ten virgins (Matthew 25:1-13), the parable of the talents (Matthew 25:14-30) and the parable of the sheep and the goats (Matthew 25:31-46) together are the parables of judgement which bring to an end not only this passage of teaching on the things of the future, but complete everything but the Passion Narrative. The belief in judgement is profoundly Jewish, often closely associated with the belief in the vindication of the faithful. Together these parables explore this theme, and highlight the seriousness of the present moment. Between them they face those who hear them with the eternal significance of their actions. Matthew not only has in mind those who heard of Jesus but did not believe in him; at this stage in the Gospel, he is also placing in front of his readers their responsibility for both believing in and following Jesus, having been given the great body of teaching contained in this Gospel. The parable of the sheep and the goats seems to go furthest in placing before his readers that any failure of love or care towards any of the faithful is a failure of love and care towards Christ. It is a solemn end to the main body of the Gospel, but it also reminds us of the great seriousness with which Matthew came to writing his Gospel. For him, discipleship is a serious business. The choice is ours:

> '*Truly I tell you: anything you failed to do for one of these, however insignificant, you failed to do for me'. And they will go away to eternal punishment, but the righteous will enter eternal life.*' (Matthew 25:45 and 46)

The Passion Narrative

In all the Gospels the Passion Narrative stands out. Here is the heart of the matter, and it is told with enormous care and detail – the longest piece of continuous narrative, no matter which Gospel we look at. Matthew is no different. It follows the Passion Narrative of St Mark's Gospel very closely, and yet in chapter 26 there is only one verse that is not in some way changed.

Matthew remains the author of everything he writes, and puts his own stamp on each episode even when he is following the order widely accepted in the Church for which he was writing. His account of the events leading up to the crucifixion does not quite stand on its own, as Mark's does; Matthew makes some effort to link it to what has gone before. As elsewhere Matthew is less direct than the earlier Gospel – the opening verses of the two Passion Narratives illustrate this well: *'It was two days before the festival of Passover and Unleavened Bread.'* (Mark 14:1) When Jesus had finished all these discourses he said to his disciples, *"You know that in two days' time it will be Passover, when the Son of Man will be handed over to be crucified"*. (Matthew 26:1 and 2)

The presentation of the Passion may be different, but in so many ways it is the same story. Matthew begins by presenting the main parties to the drama which will unfold, and the purposes they bring to their participation in the events to come. All are brought together by the celebration of Passover, which also acts as a theological backcloth – suggesting meaning, and God's participation in the drama. The ancient Passover brought freedom to the Children of Israel and began a journey to the Promised Land. Matthew would hope that in his Passion Narrative his readers would perceive God once again acting to set people free, this time from sin and the curse of death, and opening up to all who believe his new Promised Land in the shape of the kingdom to come.

The move to arrest Jesus and put him to death could not have been put in motion at a higher level: a meeting at the High Priest's residence, with the chief priests and elders of the people present, is not a casual conversation. Such a response to the things Jesus had been saying and doing is not surprising; the rift between Jesus and the authorities was as complete as it could be.

Jesus is among friends when an unexpected incident highlights tensions among those who are with him. A woman, possibly not one of the inner group, approaches Jesus and pours perfume over his head. The action takes everyone by surprise, and the response is immediate. They see it as waste; the woman intended it as an act of worship and thanksgiving. They pronounce judgement; Jesus accepts her act of love and gratitude, and gives it a meaning she probably had not intended. He has in mind the death he is destined to die – her action is so like the anointing which takes place as part of the ritual of death.

Judas is to be the man to make the first move: he detaches himself from Jesus and the other eleven, and offers the chief priests an opportunity they cannot refuse. Whether greed is his sole motive we shall never know, but the way Matthew describes the transaction suggests that money might well have been the driving force.

Passover comes closer, and the disciples go at Jesus' bidding to make arrangements in the city. Matthew is a little vague about Jesus' directions - he certainly does not mention a man carrying a jar of water! But the message they are to deliver to the householder is clear enough, and all is ready for Passover when Jesus arrives with his disciples in the evening. The Passover meal is a moving and solemn occasion for Jews, as the first Passover is remembered and the story told; living again that historical moment has great power – yet none of this is mentioned. What takes centre stage is Jesus' shock announcement that it is one of the Twelve who will betray him – with so many enemies, who could have guessed that it would be one of the inner circle who would do this? It is a painful truth for them all: for Jesus, who has given so much, but finds his love and trust repaid in this way; for the disciples, because hope is being overwhelmed by uncertainty, and in their questioning (the sign of uncertainty) their concern is about themselves, not Christ who is to be the victim. Finally, Matthew tells of Judas responding to what Jesus has announced, and the answer he receives may well hint to Judas that Jesus actually knows who will betray him.

When the Jews held the first Passover, it was to be a meal of roasted lamb and their bread was to be unleavened. They were instructed to place the blood of the lamb on the doorpost of the house, so that the angel of death would pass over that house and not touch those who were there (Exodus 12). With this as a living backcloth, Jesus acts. The meal is already well underway and the traditional reliving of the first Passover may well have been completed when Jesus takes bread, blesses and breaks it, and gives it to the disciples with the words, '*Take this and eat; this is my body.*' (Matthew 26:26) He will have broken bread to begin a meal many times before; a familiar action is given new meaning; now it is applied to him and the destiny he is to live out. The breaking is violent, but it is done so that they all can share what he gives. The cup follows – blessed and offered to them all. The significance of it could hardly be greater – a new covenant – forgiveness of sins, and so restoration of the right relationship between God and his people. By his vow of abstinence, Jesus dedicates himself to what lies ahead.

The traditional pattern of events is restored for a moment. They sing a hymn, and make their way out to the Mount of Olives in order to spend the night in the 'greater Jerusalem,' as required of those keeping the feast. On the way Jesus tells the disciples that they '*will lose faith*' and he quotes scripture to confirm that this is no accident. Peter the faithful will have none of it, but Jesus prophesies that before the night is out he will be Peter the unfaithful.

Almost lost in this difficult exchange are Jesus' words: *'after I am raised, I shall go ahead of you into Galilee.'* (Matthew 26:32) Neither failure nor death will break the bond between them.

The time in the Garden of Gethsemane and the arrest are told much as they are in St Mark's Gospel, but Matthew remains the author in the way he describes the events, what is said and what is done. For Jesus it remains a time of agony and prayer, and he asks for the support of his closest followers – but does not get it. The big meal (roast lamb would have been a rarity), the hour and the wine together means that sleep is all but overwhelming; even Peter cannot help himself. It may also have been the case that despite all that has been said, the disciples still do not understand what is about to happen. Only at the arrest does Matthew add to the traditional account of what happened: *'Do you suppose that I cannot appeal for help to my Father, and at once be sent more than twelve legions of angels? But how then would the scriptures be fulfilled, which say that this must happen?'* (Matthew 26:53 and 54) The only omission is the young man who runs away naked to avoid arrest.

The trial, if trial it was, in front of the High Priest and the Council is as unsatisfactory as ever, and turns on the moment when the High Priest addresses Jesus directly: *'By the living God I charge you to tell us: are you the Messiah, the Son of God?'* (Matthew 26:63) Jesus answers on his own terms: *'The words are yours. But I tell you this: from now on you shall see the Son of Man seated at the right hand of the Almighty and coming on the clouds of heaven.'*
Jesus' answer is in the terms of Daniel, chapter 7 which the Council will have recognised. He makes it clear that it is he who will fulfil the prophecy of scripture, and any decision they make will be made in the clear knowledge of who he is. This is the moment of truth; it is also the moment of rejection, and they give their verdict: *'He is guilty; he should die.'* With this the violence towards Jesus begins.

Peter's ordeal is about to start. By comparison it is almost incidental – a casual remark from a serving-girl. But Peter is in a situation for which he is not prepared, and everything takes him by surprise; the damage is done before he realises it. Only the sound of cockcrow brings him to his senses, and the tears come.

Matthew makes his own contributions before his account of Jesus' trial before Pilate and his crucifixion. The story of Judas' remorse, his returning of the money and his suicide are only found in Matthew's Gospel – so too the actions of the chief priests in buying the potter's field and the quotation from Jeremiah. At such a pivotal moment it is a strange dwelling on things that were so much at the periphery of the central action – but this is Matthew, the Scribe, being careful about even the smallest matter, as the law would have required.

There are also little touches about the trial before Pilate which give Matthew's account its own particular flavour. The bandit was called Jesus Barabbas – so the choice was between the Jesus of violence (the son of his father) or Jesus the Messiah, who is facing trial because he acknowledged himself to be the Son of God. To this Matthew adds the message to Pilate from his wife: *'Have nothing to do with that innocent man.'* (Matthew 27:19) In the end it was not truth or justice which won the day; political expediency (and his own skin) led Pilate to wash his hands of the whole business; the chief priests and elders have got their way. Matthew adds the chilling response of the crowd: *'His blood be on us and on our children.'* (Matthew 27:26)

Few elements in Matthew's presentation of the crucifixion are different from the earlier Gospel's account. His text is not as starkly brief as the narrative in St Mark's Gospel, and so lacks some of the bleakness of Mark chapter 15. The course of events is much the same: the game of 'King' was quite a common feature of such executions, but it is told here because it underlines what is true of Jesus; Simon is pressed into service to carry Jesus' cross, but Matthew goes no further in identifying him than simply naming his home town. It is words of mockery by the passers-by and the chief priests where Matthew has added his own contribution: *'If you really are the Son of God,'* and *'for he said he was God's Son.'* (Matthew 27:40 and 43) This is the great truth that they reject, yet it is exactly this truth which sets him apart and gives this crucifixion its unique power and importance. Matthew records the darkness and the words of desolation from Psalm 22, as well as the sour joke about Elijah. All is waiting for the final moment. When it comes it is accompanied by extraordinary signs: *'the earth shook, rocks split, and graves opened; many of God's saints were raised from sleep, and coming out of their graves after his resurrection entered the Holy City, where many saw them.'* (Matthew 27:51-53)

To express the significance of the moment Matthew reaches into the scriptures, and uses the way they had symbolically talked about God's unique activity. This is the moment when Jesus' destiny is fulfilled. The tearing of the curtain of the Temple signifies the end of the Temple as the focus of God's presence among his people, and the centurion, who has watched it all gave his witness: *'This must have been a son of God.'* (Matthew 27:54)

Throughout his account of the crucifixion, at no stage does Matthew make any reference to the pain and suffering that Jesus endures. His mind is on other things – not because the suffering is not very real, but because in such a brutal event it would be possible to lose sight of the dimension which gives this moment its eternal significance. Even in a factual description, Matthew is determined that his readers shall not forget for one moment that it is as Son of God that Jesus accepts the cup laid upon him by the Father.

The burial happens speedily – but not without witnesses. Matthew, however, has one more element he needs to cover. It may well have been that the Christian community had had their account of the resurrection dismissed – 'They came at night and stole the body!' He includes the placing of the guard at the graveside to head off any such suggestion, and conveniently the guards also become part of the evidence that the resurrection did take place.

Resurrection and beyond

Matthew was never going to be satisfied with a straight description of the events of the first Easter day. The raising of Jesus is a divine act of great power; it needs to be told in terms that do justice to the nature of the moment. So again, earthquakes and an angel whose face shone like lightning and whose garments were white as snow, and a gesture of victory (with the angel rolling away the stone and sitting on it) are the ways in which he chooses to portray the victory and the triumph of the resurrection of Christ. For those on the spot, nothing would have been more convincing than the appearance of the risen Jesus himself, and this happens as they make their way to tell the disciples what they had seen and heard. Matthew almost seems bent on making sure that the things not touched upon in St Mark's Gospel are recorded. More important for him is to bring this Gospel to the glorious conclusion he planned. Other great figures of scripture were usually afforded a great final pronouncement which spoke of the future and great things to come. Matthew plans this for his own work of scripture. But before he can do that, he has to follow through the story of what happened to the guard placed around the grave by the Jewish authorities. It is sad that a grubby little story of bribery and deception should need to be included, and as he points out, the story was in circulation when he was writing, and it was essential that an answer is placed on record.

The final words of the Gospel bring us to the conclusion he had planned. Once again they are on a mountaintop, and at his appearance the disciples '*knelt in worship.*' Nothing has been omitted which would give Jesus' final words (and the final words of the Gospel) the awe-inspiring setting they deserve: '*Full authority in heaven and on earth has been committed to me. Go therefore to all nations and make them my disciples; baptize them in the name of the Father, and the Son and the Holy Spirit, and teach them to observe all that I have commanded you. I will be with you always, to the end of time.*' (Matthew 28:18-20)

Jesus speaks as the King who has come into his Kingdom. This is the first element of the completion. At the beginning of the Gospel the birth was announced of the *'new-born king of the Jews.'* By dying and rising Jesus becomes not only the King of the Jews; he is King over all people for all time. There is no limit to his authority or the dimensions of his Kingdom. The promise given by the prophets is realised at this moment. This is the King who has given new commands to his disciples. They fulfil and complete the commandments given on Sinai, and his followers have the responsibility both to live out these commands and teach them to others. Matthew, the Scribe, intends what he has written to set out these commands which every disciple will read and learn and put into action. On his authority, baptism is to replace circumcision as a sign of membership, and by the time he wrote, the formula by which people were baptised had become established as baptism *'in the name of the Father, and the Son and the Holy Spirit,'* and this is incorporated in Jesus' final words.

Final reflection on this Gospel

The Gospel according to St Matthew has its own purpose and nature, and has made its own particular contribution to the life and witness of the Church. By some it has been thought of as the 'Jewish Gospel' – but it is a great deal more than that. Its author put pen to paper when the life of the Church was becoming more settled, and needed a scripture of its own which would enable the Christian community to be more focused and coherent both in its life and witness. His sources were both oral and written, but his contribution was to see that there needed to be a core document which would allow the Christian faith-community to have a separate existence from the Jewish faith. His own experience in the Jewish community – probably born and brought up within it, and so understanding how scripture worked and what it needed to be in order to enable it to fulfil the unique role of scripture – set the parameters of what he set out to write; Jesus – experiences and memories of him – filled its content. This Gospel treads a delicate path, valuing the Old Testament, but longing to lead its readers beyond the limits of the old to embrace the new reality personified by Jesus. It had its own time and place in the development of the young Church. The Christian faith-community was probably not yet thinking in terms of scripture; it was the forward-looking insight of the writer of this Gospel which provided it with this vital resource which enabled the Church to move on beyond its Jewish origins and become a world faith. We should be eternally grateful for the role it played in this transition.

There is, however, more to celebrate in this Gospel. It provides a particular kind of material which informs and instructs the individual and the community in the living out of its discipleship in Christ; the Sermon on the Mount has a stature all its own. For that alone – but there is so much more – this Gospel is priceless, and plays its role still in educating, guiding and inspiring those who seek to live the Christian life. Within its pages there is material which we find nowhere else – some of the great parables near the end of the Gospel speak still with great power – and we are the richer for them having been included.

St Matthew's Gospel should be allowed to stand in its own right, not in comparison with others, but as an original and authentic witness to Christ, son of David, son of Abraham and Son of God. As a Gospel it is irreplaceable.

CHAPTER FOUR

Luke – Man of the World and Apologist

It is remarkable to think that we might actually know something about the man who has given us the Gospel according to St Luke. If we are right to conclude that the author is to be identified as *'dear friend Luke, the doctor'* (Colossians 4:14), then we can also be sure that many of the events and confrontations which are recorded in the latter part of the Acts of the Apostles have also been part of the author's experience. The coincidence is rather more than incidental. The author will have had first-hand experience of how difficult it was to make the Christian case in a world that was often hostile to the new faith. Paul's experience of officialdom – not least magistrates and governors – may well have influenced the author of the Gospel, and in later years made him determined to set out the Christian story so that there might be rather more understanding of the 'Way' than the redoubtable Paul had found. Time and again, Paul had been arrested and imprisoned, yet it was violence against Paul and his companions which had usually prompted such action.

Setting out a case to establish that followers of Jesus were not subversive is one thing; what Luke has given us in the two volumes of his 'apologia' is rather more. There is no understanding the Christian 'Way' without also knowing about the Jesus Christians follow, and the way the faith came into existence. But as the Gospel progresses, it is increasingly clear that Luke's hope to inform and persuade also becomes a record which invites faith. While he does not seek to engage his audience in the same manner as the Gospel according to St Mark, his presentation of his subject is both engaging and attractive. He makes it possible for his readers not only to understand and have sympathy with the followers of Jesus; the Jesus he presents invites a response, first of approval, then of faith. Luke may have started with the idea of 'setting the record straight,' but it may well be that his purpose in writing expanded, and in the end his two-volume work is Gospel and Apologia all rolled into one.

It may not be possible to prove conclusively that the writer is Luke, the doctor, but a great deal fits, and we must take these factors into account when we turn to the Gospel itself and listen to what it tells us. What is certain is that the author looked to the Gentile world for the tools he needed to do the job. He looks to the world of secular study, not Jewish scripture, to give him the form required to begin his account. He takes seriously the approach usually used by such studies, researching personally the subject – not just relying on the accounts of others. While a considerable amount of material is still alive in the faith community, he goes beyond what others have done so as to give an ordered and authentic account of what has taken place. The writer is literate and widely read; he is thoroughly at home in the Roman world of his day. His work is addressed to those beyond the Jewish world who may well be encountering Jesus and the Christian 'Way' for the first time. He treads an entirely different path from Matthew and Mark, but he has a voice which equally deserves to be heard.

Birth stories

The Gospel begins with not one birth story but two. Both of them are miraculous and unexpected, both are begun by an encounter with an angel, and both contain material for which there is no parallel anywhere else in the Gospels (indeed the New Testament). From the beginning, Jesus and John the Baptist are linked, and that remains true throughout the Gospel. Forerunner and Saviour are born at God's initiative; in each case an angel brings the message of God's intention, and spells out the respective roles those who are to be born will play.

But Luke is careful to ground his story in the world for which he is writing, and he begins his account with a date – *'In the reign of King Herod of Judaea'* (Luke 1:5). It may not be the most precise date to twenty-first century minds, but in Luke's day it was all that was expected. By doing this he is signalling to his readers that however exceptional the account that is to follow, this is to be understood as something that took place, and is to be trusted as the starting point for the events which will unfold. There is a pattern in the encounter between Zachariah and the angel which will soon be repeated: the appearance of the angel prompted fear, to which the angel responds with the words, *'Do not be afraid,'* and then spells out God's promise of a child who will have a unique part to play in the working out of God's plan. Zachariah, understandably, voices his doubts (doubts he must have rehearsed to himself so many times, even as he prayed for a child), but this is a plan that not even doubt will defeat, and Zachariah finds himself dumbfounded (literally) and can explain to no one what has happened.

Zachariah's meeting with the angel is followed six months later by the angel's visit to Mary. If the pattern of the meeting is much the same, the response is different; Mary wonders at what she is told and questions come into her mind as well, but it is her calm acceptance of what the angel said which gives this moment an entirely different tone. Soon Mary sets out to visit her cousin Elizabeth, and the two share their astonishing secret. Luke's account is so personal and uncomplicated that we are given more than simply an account of what happened. We are being brought very close to the responses of both women to the role God has given them: Mary's song of praise (Luke 1:46-55) speaks for both of them as she gives voice to her wonder at what God is doing. This is the first of three hymns which Luke gives us. Each is very much in the form of a psalm, the Jewish form of hymn, which for centuries had expressed the inner joys and sorrows, longings and agonies of the faithful. Mary's hymn does exactly that, but while the form is Jewish (and echoes Hannah's prayer in 1 Samuel 2:1 to 10) the Greek is very much Luke's. It may well be that he translated into Greek an Aramaic original which he discovered during his researches. What he gives us is a joyful and wondering hymn of praise, expressing a very personal response to what God is doing.

The three hymns, all of which are to be found in these first two chapters of St Luke's Gospel, have their own place still in the worship of the Church. As the Magnificat, the Benedictus and the Nunc Dimittis they have been part of the Daily Offices of the Church for centuries, and have given Christians of every generation words of praise and wonder to enrich worship from great cathedrals to tiny parish Churches.

Mary, in her song of praise, delights in the action of God as he has turned upside down the way of the world. This is not just a feature of his choice of Mary and Elizabeth; it is to be a feature of the whole of the Gospel story, and we shall find this reflected in teaching and events throughout St Luke's Gospel.

The first birth is that of John the Baptist, and the delightful story of the confusion about what the baby is to be called is hardly the kind of thing to be invented. Zachariah has the last word on what his son is to be called, and at last he finds his voice. His song of praise is the song of a man of God, steeped in the faith and hopes of the Jewish people. Anyone reading this hymn, even if they are not familiar with the history of the Jewish people, will be given a clear picture of the longings and expectations which stand behind the events that are beginning to unfold. The purpose of the hymn, however, is not information but praise and thanksgiving to God, whose intervention has brought about this most unexpected birth. Zachariah's words near the end of the hymn spell out the role his son is to fulfil: *'And you, my child, will be called Prophet of the Most High, for you will be the Lord's forerunner, to prepare his way and lead his people to a knowledge of salvation.'* (Luke 1:76)

The birth of Jesus also begins with a date, and Luke places what is to take place firmly in the life of the known world. Joseph and Mary find themselves caught up in a census which Luke tells us took place throughout the Roman Empire. They were in Bethlehem when Mary's time came, and an inspired piece of improvisation by Joseph meant that there was at least some shelter for the birth to happen. Of all the Gospel writers, it is only Luke who tells us anything about the birth, another original fruit of his researches, and the image of a stable – *'because there was no room for them at the inn'* has been the prism through which the birth of Christ has been seen ever since. The human poverty of the birth is in contrast to the songs of the angels which greeted the birth, and just as the birth happened on the edge of society, so the good news is shared with people who also are on the edge – men whose way of life is not shared by most of society, and so are often regarded with suspicion if not disdain.

The rituals of birth run their course. Jesus is circumcised, and after forty days Mary and Joseph find themselves in the Temple for the rites of purification. Luke gives his Gentile audience chapter and verse for the rituals that take place, but the whole event is interpreted when Simeon takes the baby in his arms. His hymn of recognition and praise has a feel of completion about it – not just Simeon's vigil, waiting for God to fulfil his promises, but the waiting of the whole people for the promised time to come. With the arrival of this child the waiting is over – and this too is recognised in what God has brought about. Simeon's words are confirmed by Anna, a prophetess, and all this takes place in the Temple which is the very centre of the Jewish faith.

In just a few verses Jesus is back there again, but now a twelve-year-old who is learning and asking questions – perhaps quite unaware of the things that had been said twelve years before. Those intervening years Luke notes briefly in a very general way. While many long to know more, Luke does not indulge us. He wants us to see the link between the things that were said and done all those years ago, and the actions of Jesus – his first conscious actions recorded – as a young man beginning to develop in the way the Spirit is leading him. We may sympathise with Mary and Joseph in their anxiety, but Luke is concentrating on Jesus and the way he feels impelled to be *'in my Father's house'* (Luke 2:49). This episode ends with a note of Mary's response: as she had after the visit of the shepherds in Bethlehem, Mary *'treasured up all these things in her heart.'* It is such a personal response, but it also gives Luke the opportunity to underscore that all he has said about the birth of Jesus comes from Mary. What a contrast with Matthew who approached his account of the birth through the mind and actions of Joseph.

Preparations for ministry

The next stage in Luke's presentation begins with the fullest of all possible dates. Both the political and the religious sides of life are represented, and show us the very considerable care Luke is taking in order to set out an authoritative and well-grounded account of events. Even though his account has included angels and miraculous births, everything is rooted in historical fact and its place on the world scene can be precisely identified.

Before the Messiah can be brought centre-stage, the work of the forerunner must be given its proper place. John's authority is rooted in scripture, but Luke includes not just the first few words from Isaiah which are quoted in the other Gospels. He makes sure that the scope of his ministry is not limited and local: *'and all mankind shall see God's deliverance'* (Luke 3:6). In the same way his ministry is not just limited to his prophetic action of baptism: this firebrand of a man challenged everyone, religious and non-religious, Jews and non-Jews – even Herod came under his judgement, and this led to John being thrown into prison. But John is quite clear: he is neither Saviour nor Messiah for all the power of his ministry. He calls all who come to him to look forward: *'But there is one coming who is mightier than I am. I am not worthy to unfasten the straps of his sandals.'*

Only after this is the baptism of Jesus recorded (in two verses). It is hardly presented as a moment of high significance: the baptism was a general baptism; Jesus had been baptised and was praying; only then does *'heaven open and the Holy Spirit descended on him in bodily form like a dove, and there came a voice from heaven, "You are my beloved Son; in you I delight".'* This is the moment of great significance, even if it almost seems to get lost in all we are being told about John. Luke's account may not have the drama of Mark or the public proclamation of Matthew, but from this moment on Jesus has the assurance of God's love and favour; the Spirit too is with him to begin his life's work and to bring into reality all that God has promised. From now on the storyline will follow Jesus, for he is the person to whom John has been pointing. So Luke takes pains to give some more background to Jesus, tracing his family tree, not just back to Abraham, but to Adam – the first man. Jesus belongs to the whole human race.

One more element of preparation must happen before the ministry can begin – a time of testing, a confrontation with the tempter himself. This account of the encounter with the tempter looks so similar to Matthew's, but there are differences. Luke takes the tests in a different order; he shortens the first text of scripture, and presents each test in a slightly different way. Such changes would only have become significant after the accounts were written down. It is the same story being told, but in other words and with a different emphasis. This may simply be the way the story, possibly still in an oral form, came to Luke; there seems not to be any deliberate rewriting of Matthew in the way Luke presents the event. This may well be true throughout the Gospel when events are written up with minor variations: so different are both the sources and the audiences that it is inevitable that the authors will express their accounts differently. What is important is to be alert to the particular emphasis that each is giving in his record. Our expectations have largely been shaped by our use of written texts; we expect agreement, which is only made possibly by being able to copy word for word what is written. But we have already seen enough in the first three chapters to realise that Luke has discovered a great deal of fresh material, most of which must have been oral in nature.

The question behind each of the tests is: 'How shall you use your undoubted powers?' In the first test, Jesus gives a crisp reply: his powers are not for personal convenience, and his use of words of scripture indicate that he will use his power to do God's will rather than being self-serving. So too, when it comes to questions of power – the kind of King he will be – he rejects the pattern which the world presents in order to serve and glorify the Father, who is God. Should he use his power to provide miraculous proof of who he is? Such demonstrations as the tempter suggests are empty – and not 'of God.' Jesus rejects the tempter's way in favour of a Son's obedience to the Father's will, and at every turn the words of God in scripture set out the way he should go.

Ministry in Galilee

Luke opens his account of Jesus' ministry with a very general picture of how it all began. At this point, there are no disciples, just wide approval for all he was doing, but at the very first event which Luke recalls in detail Jesus encounters opposition and disbelief. He might not have expected this in his hometown where he had grown up, but what began with murmurs of approval became, firstly, hostile and then dangerous. There are, however, features of this event which need to be explored. All the best stories flow from beginning to end, and it is possible to follow their development with ease. Not only does this story tell of Jesus' visit to the town where he grew up very differently from the other Gospels; there is a moment when there is a hiatus – new material is introduced which does not blend in with the original story, and takes it in a new direction. A great deal must have happened, which is not included in the way the story is told, to move the storyline from 'general approval,' to the point when Jesus quotes the proverb, *Physician, heal yourself!'* (Luke 4:23). Jesus is clearly responding to a change in mood around him, and the way he builds his response indicates that there was questioning, doubt, even disbelief that one of their own could do what he had been reported as doing elsewhere. None of this is mentioned, but it is essential for understanding the new direction of the story; it is a surprising direction, but one which fits with a Gentile audience, not necessarily the people of Nazareth who take their hostility to the point of danger to Jesus. His own folks had not offered him any recognition; they simply could not see him as a man of God, a prophet. In this he was like Elijah and Elisha who in their day found recognition beyond the bounds of Israel.

The way this story has developed tells us a great deal about what to expect as the Gospel continues. Luke is not only familiar with the story we have heard in Mark and Matthew; he also has other material which he works into what becomes a very different story. In doing this, essential elements of one story are missed out at the point when other parts of another story are grafted in. Luke will do this again and again in the course of the Gospel, and the joins are not always smooth: they often leave the original story greatly changed. Luke has a reputation of being a great storyteller; it is probably more appropriate to say that he tells many magnificent stories, but his use of the scalpel in trimming and reshaping the material he has is not always seamless. We should also note how aware he is of the audience for whom he is writing; that too greatly shapes his choice of material and how it is handled.

This complicated scenario should not take away from the magnificent text from Isaiah which stands at the beginning of the episode. It is a glorious proclamation of the nature and purpose of Jesus' mission: *'The spirit of the Lord is upon me because he has anointed me'* (Luke 4:18); this has been the significance of the gift of the Spirit after his baptism. All he says and does is empowered by God; he is sent by God to bring good news, release, healing and freedom to all those who carry the burdens of life. It is a marvellous manifesto of mercy and hope which is rooted and grounded in the power and purposes of God. It is to be the Lord's Jubilee, when life is given a new beginning, and wholeness and hope is given to those who suffer. Jesus will live out this manifesto in word and action; that is how we are to understand the ministry which begins with this event.

Luke now launches into the ministry of Jesus, and a familiar pattern begins to emerge. They are in Capernaum, and his preaching on the Sabbath prompts recognition; there is real authority in what he says. Then he is challenged by a man in the grip of a demon, and the same authority is recognised in what he does: *'What is there in this man's words? He gives orders to the unclean spirits with authority and power and they go'* (Luke 4:36). Luke is following Mark's pattern, but the feel of the stories is entirely different. Luke is reporting from a distance; the events are the same, but the language and the point of view from which they are told are altogether different; most of the material he includes from the oral tradition represented by Mark has the same treatment – with some interesting results.

After the synagogue, they go to Simon's house – this is the first mention of Simon; he is not yet (officially) a disciple; his calling, and that of the other fishermen, is yet to come. The healing of the sick at sunset completes a busy day. What we notice, in passing, is that there seems to be no objection to Jesus healing on the Sabbath; that is a controversy to come. For the moment, Jesus remains on his own, so when he is found at prayer in a remote spot the next day, he is free to move on, though the note that he preached in the synagogues of Judaea is a bit of a surprise; Capernaum is in Galilee, and the next event begins beside the *'lake of Gennesaret'* (Luke 5:1).

The short stories which ended chapter 4, for which there are parallels in Mark 1, are reported in an almost disengaged manner. The call of Peter (still called Simon at this stage) is in complete contrast. While those stories are from what might have been for Luke a widely-known tradition, the story Luke now tells is direct, dramatic and very powerful. It is, perhaps, inevitable that Luke uses his different sources in quite distinct ways, and at this point his style and language are sufficiently different to suggest that the stories of the miraculous draught of fish and the call of Peter are the product of his researches. Perhaps the only meeting-point between this story and the account of Peter's call in Mark 1 is to be seen in Jesus' words: *'From now on you will be catching people'* (Luke 5:10). But Luke's researches have given us a gem. How do you challenge a person like Simon, the fisherman? The only thing he knows about is fishing – and even he is not always successful. As the story unfolds, the fisherman finds himself confronted in the only terms he understands – fishing. It is not words or arguments which speak to Peter, but he is in no doubt about the meaning of the great shoal of fish they catch. His first reaction is to try to push Jesus away from him; but this is to be a life-changing moment, and with Jesus' encouragement he makes his response – as do the other fishermen involved in the great catch.

From the intensity of the fishing trip which changed lives, Luke returns to his usual, but more distant, manner of reporting events. We have already noted that when he is handling the material from the traditional source oddities sometimes creep in; the healing of the leper illustrates this. It is inconceivable that a leper would have been openly in a town, such was the fear of the disease; and Luke ends the story with crowds coming to Jesus in ever greater numbers, not with Jesus having to stay in the open country. In this way, Luke seems to reverse the ending of the story of the healing of the leper. Perhaps he understands the importance of Jesus being able to heal even a leper, and tells of great crowds coming to Jesus as the only fitting response to someone with such power.

Luke follows the traditional order of things with a story about the healing of a paralysed man, but such is his freedom in handling his material that he changes both the details of the event and the order in which they are presented. Luke's story begins with Jesus' audience – Pharisees and teachers of the law; in his mind, at least, the importance of Jesus' reply to the challenge of these religious experts is possibly far greater than the details of the healing – remarkable though it was. The message Luke wants to communicate to his readers is summed up in verse 24: *'But to convince you that the Son of Man has the right on earth to forgive sins.'* The healing of the man is evidence that Jesus speaks a truth which is beyond all their expectations – *'The things we have seen today are beyond belief'* – and in the light of what they have seen it is those expectations which must change.

Luke does not use the Sea of Galilee as a focus for Jesus' ministry in quite the same way as Mark, so the call of Levi is introduced differently, though the story is in essence much the same, as is the clash with the Pharisees. Luke does not make quite such a point as Mark does about the characters of those who came to the party at Levi's house, but the point is the same: *'I have not come to call the virtuous but sinners to repentance'* (Luke 5:32). Christ has come to bring change. The godly should be able to recognise who Jesus is and what he is doing; it is those whose way of life leads them away from God who are the people who need to have their direction in life changed; that is what Jesus is about.

The question of fasting is put in a much more general way: what makes fasting inappropriate, for the moment, is the presence of Jesus and the urgent task he and his followers have been given. Jesus is not ignoring the call of God for obedience and dedication; it is in obedience to God that they work now. The time for waiting on God, and praying for the coming of the kingdom belongs to another time. Jesus is not denying the place and importance of fasting; he simply says 'This is not the time.'

The two small parables – about a new patch and new wine – both have adjustments made to them – to the point at which the meaning of the parables

1 Picture of St Aidan of Lindisfarne

'How are they to hear without a preacher?' *(***Romans 10:14***)*

This striking statue of Aidan stands today on Holy Island (Lindisfarne) for all to see. He is looking south – towards the ruins of the Priory and beyond to Bamburgh Castle. Aidan came with a group of Monks at the request of Oswald, King of Northumbria, and so began the Golden Age of Northumbria. The ruins we see today come from a much later time – the Priory Church itself was modelled on Durham Cathedral. It was a wooden Church which Aidan and his companions built, and it was in this place that the glorious Lindisfarne Gospels were created.

Aidan was not the first to come from Iona, but his love for the poor and care for those he met meant that his message of Christ and God's love was readily received. He died at nearby Bamburgh in 651 AD.

2. St Matthew's Gospel

St Matthew begins his Gospel: 'The genealogy of Jesus Christ, son of David, son of Abraham.' **(Matthew 1:1)**

Pictures from the Lindisfarne Gospels:
The Lindisfarne Gospels are part of the flowering of the Golden Age of Northumbria. The extraordinary intricacy of design in some of the pages reproduced in this book (with permission from the British Library) has few equals.

3. St Mark's Gospel

'The beginning of the gospel of Jesus Christ the Son of God.' (**Mark 1:1**)

The images on the cover of this book bring together the cover pages of each Gospel which depict each Gospel-writer with his symbol (Matthew the figure of a Man; Mark the figure of a Lion; Luke the figure of a Flying Ox; John the figure of an Eagle).

4. St Luke's Gospel

'To Theophilus: Many writers have undertaken to draw up an account of the events that have taken place among us, following the traditions handed down to us by the original eyewitnesses and servants of the gospel. So I in my turn, as one who has investigated the whole course of these events in detail, have decided to write an orderly narrative for you, your excellency, so as to give you authentic knowledge about the matters of which you have been informed.'

(Luke 1:1-4)

The pages inside present us with the first pages of Gospel text. In each, the first words of each Gospel are elaborately decorated and presented in great detail. It is a mark of the great veneration in which these Gospels were held that such care and skill was lavished on their presentation.

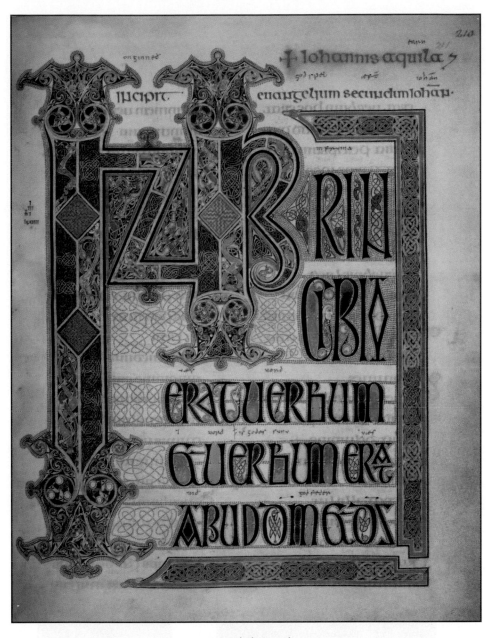

5. St John's Gospel

'In the beginning the Word already was. The Word was in God's presence, and what God was,
the Word was.' **(John 1:1)**

They were, it seems, the work of one man, Eadfrith, who was Bishop of Lindisfarne from 698 to 721. They were created in honour of Cuthbert who died in 687. It seems almost impossible for the Gospels to have survived, but we have them to marvel at and to learn what high value should rightly be given to the Gospels.

6. Rothwell (Ruthwell) Cross

This magnificent Anglo-Saxon Cross now stands in an apse in Rothwell Church. It stands 18 feet high, and is perhaps one of the most elaborate Anglo-Saxon monumental sculptures known to us. It is believed to date from the 8th century in what was then part of the Kingdom of Northumbria. It was severely damaged in 1664, but restored in 1818 and moved to its present position later in the century. Pesvner writes: 'The crosses of Bewcastle and Ruthwell are the greatest achievement of their date in the whole of Europe.'

7. Bewcastle Cross

The head of the Cross is missing, but it is thought to be standing in its original position. This Cross also is thought to belong to the 8th century in what was then part of the Kingdom of Northumbria. The intricate decorations include animals, vine scrolls, knots, as well as the figures of Christ and John the Baptist. It is thought to have been one of the earliest English sundials to survive.

8. Cædmon Cross Whitby

Memorial to Cædmon, Created in imitation of the great Anglo-Saxon crosses, this cross was erected in 1898, and is to be found beside the Parish Church. It looks out over the harbour to the north and west and the ruins of Whitby Abbey to the south and east. It celebrates the connection of Cædmon, the first English poet, with Whitby Abbey where he lived and worked as Cowherd. The figures on the Cross are: Christ (hand raised in Blessing), David (the shepherd and musician) Hilda (Abbess of Whitby) and Cædmon (singing his great song).

is entirely altered! While Mark talks about the new patch shrinking and only making the original tear worse, Luke is anxious about the damage done to the new garment from which the patch was taken – and that the new material will not match! Luke makes a little addition of his own to the parable about wine and wineskins: he clearly knows a thing or two about wine, and observes that *'no one after drinking old wine wants new; for he says, "The old wine is good".'* (Luke 5:39) It is difficult to know whether Luke is trying to make a new and subtle point – 'Everyone loses when you try to mix Christianity and the Jewish faith; it just will not work' – or whether as a man of the world he makes his own observations on the subject of the original parable.

One area where the two faiths will never agree is on the question of the Sabbath. In each of the Gospels the Sabbath is a constant source of argument and disagreement. Two stories now follow (as they do in Mark) which highlight this controversy. But Luke has softened Jesus' response to the challenge from the Pharisees, compared with Mark, and omits the principle *'The Sabbath was made for man, not man for the Sabbath'* (Mark 2:27) and so takes away the reason for concluding that 'The Son of Man is master of the Sabbath.' The healing of the man with the withered arm is also adjusted, and does not end with Jesus' accusers walking out and planning how to *'bring about Jesus' death'* (Mark 3:6). It may well be that the story came to Luke in this rather gentler form; more likely is the possibility that Luke has deliberately taken some of the sting out of this story for his own reasons.

The choosing of the twelve follows a time of prayer. Luke makes many more references to Jesus praying (prayer was often practised in public and out loud). Frequently in this Gospel it is a prelude to a moment of decision or action. What Luke also adds to the traditional account of the choosing of the Twelve is to call them 'Apostles' – although this is a role they do not really take up until after the gift of the Spirit at Pentecost. (This may be a small insight into the way Luke thought of them, and a reminder to us that he is thinking beyond the scope of the Gospel even at this early stage). He has adjusted the order of events in a very minor way, and uses his version of the great crowd which came to Jesus to provide him with the ideal setting in which to give the first real body of teaching in this Gospel. We cannot help noticing the very different introduction Luke gives to his 'Sermon', known by scholars as 'The Sermon on the Plain' because Jesus *'stopped on some level ground'* (Luke 6:17). Gone is the mountain, and the implied reference to Moses and God's presence, and the giving of the Ten Commandments; gone are the phrases *'in spirit,'* and *'to see right prevail'*; gone are the elements of Matthew's great Sermon which were rooted in the Jewish heritage, not least the Law. This is to be a

Sermon for Gentile ears, and is utterly down to earth – not given a timeless spiritual quality which is so distinctive of Matthew's Sermon. Jesus addresses the *'poor . . . the hungry . . . you who weep . . . you when people hate you and ostracize you . . .'* He speaks to them directly which gives the whole Sermon a different feel. The blessings Jesus pronounces stand on their head the suffering they are enduring: the 'kingdom of God' is Luke's preferred way of speaking about what God promises – a time when struggle and suffering and need are things of the past; weeping is replaced by laughter; the despised will dance for joy.

We have already seen this heady delight at what God is doing in Mary's song (Luke 1:46-55), so it is not surprising that there is a counterpart to the blessings. The four blessings are followed by four woes. All of this is part of God's great activity of turning upside down the usual way of the world. Luke is not so much trying to lay down the foundations for good Christian living, as celebrating the way God is setting free the downtrodden and bringing freedom and fullness to those denied it in the usual patterns of life. The very unexpectedness of what Jesus is announcing gives it the feel of God's promises being fulfilled – the fundamental theme of Christ's ministry which Jesus announced at his first sermon in Nazareth. It would be quite wrong to interpret the 'woes' as trying to make a moral point about the nature of riches and plenty. He might want to affirm that such material things cannot give salvation or peace or eternal life, but that is not the point of the contrast he has given us.

Anyone living under God's new dispensation also has a new way of living. The contrast with what might be considered 'normal' is startling: Christ's command is to: *'love your enemies'; 'do good to those who hate you'; 'bless those who curse you'; 'pray for those who treat you spitefully'*.

None of this is ever easy: offering love to an enemy demands courage and selflessness, looking beyond the hostility and hurt which usually accompany enmity. To act in the face of hatred requires a toughness which refuses to repay like with like. Being generous towards those who offer nothing but spite calls for a magnanimity that is almost superhuman. All these responses are the very reverse of what might be expected – but it is Christ's way: instead of exchanging blows, do the unthinkable and offer the other cheek; offer more than they ask to those who demand from you; give without seeking a return. Christ's command is not to conform to the usual expected patterns; those who follow him are given a new standard – it comes from God himself: *'Be compassionate, as your Father is compassionate.'* (Luke 6:30)

The other great command in this Sermon is: *'Do not judge.'* (Luke 6:37) Standing in judgement belongs to the way of the world; God's generous dealings with us are in complete contrast to it. Yet as soon as the disciple follows God's way, mercy and generosity bring reconciliation and the possibility of change. However simple the terms in which he lays it out, Luke is presenting a pattern of life which stands out from the world around. The short sayings that follow (verses 39-45) do not necessarily belong together – and they are not particularly religious in tone – but they mostly continue the direction Luke has established, and anyone listening to them will recognise home truths which fill out the theme of 'do not judge.' The Sermon ends in much the same way as Matthew's Sermon on the Mount; the details of the parable may differ, but the message is the same: the teaching offered in this Sermon is to be acted upon; Christ's commands are a proper foundation for life; anything less risks disaster.

The two great Sermons given us by Matthew and Luke contrast in so many ways, yet there is a pattern which they share: both writers provide a setting; both Sermons take place almost as soon as the ministry has established itself; both begin with blessings, and while the content is almost completely different, both end with the parable about foundations. Luke follows his Sermon with the healing of the centurion's servant; Matthew allows one event to intrude before he also records this event. However different their way of recording this moment, both include the words of the centurion about obedience (very apt after both Sermons) and the words of Jesus, *'I tell you, not even in Israel have I found such faith.'* (Luke 7:9) A Gentile audience would have warmed to this comment; they too are included both in Jesus' teaching and the mercy he shows.

Luke alone tells the story of Jesus restoring a dead man to life at the town of Nain. He makes us aware of the extent of the tragedy which has befallen the woman, and Jesus' readiness to respond to her need. In doing so, Jesus breaks every taboo in the book, but what is enduring about this story is the way he breaks the cold grip of death, and restores the young man to the care of his mother.

Luke makes a point of recording some of the things the crowd said in response to Jesus' action. It is the perfect setting in which to raise the question which is one step beyond the words of the crowd: *'Are you the one who is to come, or are we to expect someone else?'* (Luke 7:20) It is John the Baptist who asks the question – part of his role of pointing to Jesus as the promised Messiah – and Jesus makes his reply in the actions he is taking. John, and all those he has alerted, will recognise in his actions the fulfilment of God's promises of old. In the same way, Jesus identifies John as the expected Elijah. But Jesus does not let the moment pass without a wry comment on those who have believed and those who have rejected them: it was ordinary people, including many social outcasts who had come to believe; it was the religious devotees and the legal experts who had rejected the witness of John and Jesus (how everything is turned upside down!), albeit for opposite reasons.

In this setting, it seems particularly daring of Simon the Pharisee to invite Jesus to a meal – his fellow Pharisees would most certainly have tut-tutted at his choice of guest. But although one part of him may have wanted to find out about Jesus for himself, the Pharisee in him could not resist standing in judgement on the intruder whose way of life was known to everyone. Jesus and the Pharisee made entirely opposite responses to the actions of the woman, as Jesus' parable demonstrates, but Jesus' words to the woman are beyond all quibbling: *'Your sins are forgiven . . . Your faith has saved you; go in peace.'* (Luke 7:49 and 50)

Luke expands what he has already told us about Jesus' mission; he also tells us more about his inner circle and those who accompanied him on the mission. There were the Twelve, but there were also others, particularly women whose important role was to provide for them. They were a very mixed group, many drawn to Jesus for very individual reasons, but all had their part to play in the fellowship and the mission Jesus was engaged in. This is the setting in which Luke chooses to record the parable of the sower (Mark 4). This is quite the briefest version of the three accounts we have in the Gospels, with none of the colour of the others; even the end is rather sudden *'and yielded a hundredfold.'* Yet it is the same parable, with the same explanation – and the same reason for teaching in parables given, although with the rather puzzling quotation from Isaiah reduced. If there is an art to telling parables – to give light and understanding – there is also an art in listening; it is what the listener brings to each parable, especially a willingness to look for and respond to the message, which makes all the difference. Into this setting Luke puts the visit of Jesus' family – a visit only recorded in order for Luke to round off this section with Jesus' words, *'My mother and my brothers are those who hear the word of God and act upon it.'* (Luke 8:21)

By now, Luke has taken up the traditional order of events, and he gives his readers his own account of Jesus stilling the storm. For what was a terrifying experience, his account is extraordinarily matter-of-fact. All the elements of the story are there, but with no feel for the moment. Yet it ends with the all-important question: *'Who can this be? He gives orders to the wind and the waves, and they obey him.'* (Luke 8:26) An act of such power is followed by another event which speaks of the range of Jesus' ability to heal and restore even the most disturbed of people. Luke describes the man in his own way – it tells us something about Luke, the man, that for him the height of depravity was not wearing clothes or living in a house – but because of the way he records the event the story does not flow in quite the same way as it did in Mark. Nevertheless, the outcome is the same: fear at the power of Jesus' action from the people of the area; a wish to follow on behalf of the man who was now in his right mind.

The bringing back to life of Jairus' daughter is the third of the great actions in the traditional order, and Luke gives this story and the story of the curing of the woman who had suffered from haemorrhages their proper weight, though Luke does not mention the doctors who had treated her. What Jesus does is far beyond what others can achieve, and Luke's presentation of this event is also a challenge to his listeners to recognise what is being shown them: Jesus is no ordinary healer; he heals what others cannot cure; he raises the dead, something that only the power of God can achieve – and Luke's witness is to a God of compassion, and understanding and mercy, a side of his presentation which takes it beyond simply 'putting the record straight.'

Luke has already recorded his account of Jesus' visit to his hometown and he does not repeat it here, but he continues to follow the traditional storyline with the mission in which Jesus involved the Twelve. Even when following the account we have received in Mark, there are minor differences of expression and content which give the text a different feel. This first mission involving the disciples is part of the tapestry Luke is laying out. He is careful to choose what he includes and what he leaves aside; nothing is unthinkingly copied from his sources; he is very conscious of the different levels at which he is communicating. For this reason, if for no other, he carefully shapes how he handles the death of John the Baptist. The unedifying story of royal intrigue has no place; the fact of John the Baptist's death on the orders of Herod is simply recorded as a fact – and a fact which is overshadowed by Herod's curiosity about Jesus and his desire to see him after all that he had heard about him: *'But who is this I hear so much about?'* (Luke 9:9)

In any book, the feeding of the five thousand must stand out as one of the great moments, yet Luke's introduction is less than convincing. He tells of Jesus and the disciples who had just returned from their mission withdrawing to a town called Bethsaida, yet the disciples say to Jesus, *'Send the people off, so that they can go into the villages and farms round about to find food and lodging, for this is a remote place'*! The fundamentals of the story, however, remain: the five loaves and two fish are blessed and broken, and the disciples distribute them to the people who have been seated in groups of about fifty. *'They all ate and were satisfied'* (Luke 9:17) – a mark of God's ready provision for his people as had happened in the great Old Testament story of God feeding his people in the wilderness. This side of the story is not heavily emphasised; the account we have is for Gentile ears.

The feeding is, nevertheless, a momentous occasion – a fitting preparation for what happens next. Those who are familiar with the traditional order will be surprised at what Luke has done: gone is the walking on the water (Mark 6:45-52), the conflict with the Pharisees and the legal experts (Mark 7:1-22), the healings and the second feeding (Mark 7:24 to 8:10), the journey across the sea and the gradual healing of the blind man (Mark 8:14-26). Instead he provides a general introduction, and then plunges into the question at the heart of the Gospel: *'Who do you say I am?'* (Luke 9:20) Luke prepares us for a moment of particular importance with his note of Jesus praying, and the questions he puts to the disciples could not be more direct. General opinion is remarkable enough, yet it falls well short of the full truth about Jesus. Peter's response is as direct as the question: *'God's Messiah.'* The very words mark a turning point in this Gospel, as it has in the other two Gospels who record this moment. In Jesus all the hopes of the people, all their trust in the promises of God, become a reality – there could hardly be two more momentous words on the lips of a faithful Jew. In all the actions of Jesus, it seems the promises of God had become a reality; but what about the hopes of the people – for their hopes were shaped by being a conquered people, downtrodden by the occupying power, and constantly being reminded of it even in their own country. To say the words is one thing: to understand what they mean is another, and Jesus has to face his disciples with the true destiny he has to live out, because it is God's will. Jesus' words to his disciples would have come as a puzzling shock, and his command to silence no less mystifying – but these are truths into which they have yet to grow.

Jesus' call *'to everybody'* (Luke 9:23) is not necessarily limited to his small circle of followers to whom he has entrusted the truth about himself. He calls for discipleship which is selfless; followers who are ready to suffer for their faith; people who are going to offer him their personal loyalty in the way they live out their faith. The very reverse of what they were hoping for and expecting. Yet Jesus assures them that the kingdom will come, and it will be a present reality for those who keep the faith. We have seen nothing like this call in all the Gospel so far. Jesus speaks as the newly acknowledged Messiah; it seems to step out of the page and engage the reader as well.

What follows is no less remarkable; again prayer is part of the preparation, a mountain-top the setting; so the reader is being alerted to another moment of special importance. Luke may give a matter-of-fact report of what happened, but the whole event is shot through with symbolism and draws on the Old Testament to set before us the full meaning of the story: mountain tops speak of meeting with God; the dazzling clothes are the language of vision; Moses and Elijah are two great figures from the Old Testament associated with the coming of the Messiah; the *'departure'*, a coded reference to the way Jesus must live out his destiny in suffering and death. Peter's response would have been well understood by Luke's audience; it is not only Jews who mark such extraordinary moments by raising something which will testify to what happened in that place. It was the voice which came from the cloud which made clear the response required: *'This is my Son, my Chosen; listen to him.'* (Luke 9:35)

Throughout the first half of this Gospel, Luke has drawn on material from several different sources. It has been noticeable that when he has used the traditional source (represented by what we know as the Gospel according to St Mark) he has been almost perfunctory in the way he has handled the material. That is especially true of the next few episodes. There is no command to silence by Jesus as they come down the mountain – no amazement at Jesus' return, no argument with legal experts, no heart-rending response from the father of the boy. In essence the story is the same; Luke records it and moves on. He shortens the prophecy Jesus gives about what lies ahead; he mentions neither Jesus being killed nor the promise that he will rise again; Jesus' response to the argument about who will be the greatest makes no mention of the need to be *'last of all and servant of all'* (Mark 9:35). It is almost as if he is in a hurry to move on; Jesus must set his face towards Jerusalem and the fulfilling of his destiny.

With the beginning of the journey, there is a different feel about the episodes Luke relates. Nothing must get in Jesus' way. People must come with him or risk being left behind; there is no time for ordinary concerns as are presented to him. His uncompromising replies to two people who come to him are distinctly uncomfortable – but this is a sign of Jesus' single-mindedness: he is wholly focussed on what God has laid on him.

As part of this, Jesus initiates a new phase in the mission, and he engages a considerable number of his followers to act as his vanguard. There is more urgency and detail about his instructions when we compare them with the mission of the Twelve (Luke 9:1-6): they are to *'travel barefoot. Exchange no greeting,'* and their words and actions must fit the critical nature of the moment: *'Heal the sick there, and say "The kingdom of God has come upon you".'* People will be judged by the response they make – as will Chorazin, Bethsaida and Capernaum. When the seventy-two return we are treated to Jesus' prayer of praise to God: he sees this as a significant moment in the struggle against evil, a moment when the kingdom of God is brought a step closer. It is a moment which people who trusted God had longed to see for many a generation.

At first sight, this seems a strange moment to record one of the greatest parables that Jesus told. It stands on its own, and is not part of any sermon or body of teaching. The setting is the clue: Jesus and his disciples are announcing God's call to be part of his kingdom. Who can be part of it? *'What must I do to inherit eternal life?'* is the way the lawyer puts it. The parable does so much more than answer the question; it will not be spiritual correctness which will earn a place in the promised kingdom; to everyone the invitation goes, even to hated Samaritans; it is those who display the selfless compassion of the story's hero who will find the gates of the kingdom open to them. To have a despised Samaritan personifying the way to eternal life challenged the entrenched attitudes of Jesus' contemporaries; it has been doing that ever since.

The parable of the Good Samaritan completes the cluster of events which led up to it. The next episode acts as a preface to the sayings and teaching of the next few chapters. If over-busyness is a modern disease, it is not new, and the story of Martha and Mary strikes a chord at many levels. But for Luke this domestic episode has a more direct application. It is the hearing of and paying attention to the teaching of Jesus which is being held up as being more important than anything else. The body of teaching Luke now presents has been collected from many different places, and he weaves them into a single passage. The journey to Jerusalem is on hold while many sides of Jesus' teaching are set out. It is a very diverse passage. We recognise material and themes from Matthew's Sermon on the Mount; there are episodes from Mark, taken out of their original context but used here. There is material we have not seen before. The virtue of the written word is that it can include such diverse material without having to establish a theme or verbal connection. Luke takes advantage of this. His one purpose is to give to his readers a much wider body of teaching than he has been able to present up to this point. It is part of Luke's presentation of Jesus that he is able to show something of the breadth and depth of Jesus, the Teacher. His wisdom and insight all belong to Luke's appeal for Jesus to be respected and believed in and followed.

Once again, a note of Jesus at prayer is a starting point. It was a regular part of Jesus' life, so the request from the disciples to teach them to pray would have been quite natural. John the Baptist had taught his disciples his own prayer; the disciples ask Jesus to do the same. The prayer Luke records is almost unsettlingly short – not a word more than necessary – with none of the phrases and clauses, often of Jewish origin, which help the longer version in the Sermon on the Mount to flow. But the brevity of the prayer given here has its strengths. This is not a prayer which makes for easy recitation; it must be prayed differently. Brevity allows the one who is praying to dwell on each word, each element in turn. Perhaps it would help if it were printed differently:

> *Father, may your name be hallowed;*
> *your kingdom come.*
> *Give us each day our daily bread.*
> *And forgive us our sins,*
> *for we too forgive all who have done us wrong.*
> *And do not put us to the test.'*

The structure of the prayer is the same as the longer version: it leads the person praying into the presence of God, and allows the suppliant to centre his whole being on the Father – the Father we love, and whose presence is a delight. This leads to adoration, and the aligning of the disciple's will with the will of the Father. There is a progression of consciousness and thought, and the slower the words are said, the fuller the concentration on God. Only after this dwelling on God and his will does the disciple then place before God his needs and longings, always aware that discipleship is a living under the providence of God. In this way the Lord's Prayer becomes a model for all prayer, and can be prayed in many ways and in all circumstances. Even Jesus' prayer in Gethsemane follows this pattern, and it carried all his longings (and his obedience) to the Father. He was not hemmed in by a particular set of words – often the deepest praying is beyond words.

The teaching which follows the Lord's Prayer serves to underline how God, as Father, provides for those in his care; but there are two sides to the relationship, and the disciple must also be ready both to ask and to receive. But Luke does not stay with this theme, even though there is material later which would have fitted very well. What follows is a great mixture of sayings, Jesus often responding to criticisms and arguments going on around him. Some of the material has been recast (the parable of the strong man is told in different terms, but the meaning is the same); some material Luke may well have added (Luke 11:19 introduces a fresh argument to the traditional material about Beelzebul, which is outside of the parable format, but is very much to the point). Just as Jesus is rejected (for reasons which he shows to be wrong), so he responds by highlighting the failure of his contemporaries to recognise him, although *'What is here is greater than Solomon.'* (Luke 11:31) The Pharisees and lawyers of his day come in for particular scorn; they are the very people who should have led the recognition of Jesus. Instead they have been a barrier to it, and his constant critics. For this reason, their guilt is even greater.

In chapters 12 and 13, Luke moves beyond confrontation to direct teaching. The volume of sayings (and encounters which lead to sayings) is enormous, and such is the variety that the reader is given the feeling that all life is gathered up and spoken about. Chapter 13 ends with Jesus' moving lament over Jerusalem. The only setting which would make sense of these words is Jerusalem, but these and the many other sayings and parables which follow in the next few chapters come to us without any context – and so we are given nothing which helps us to bring some perspective to the material we are given. It may well be that this is how Luke received them, and his primary purpose is simply to record them, and so fill out the picture he is painting of Christ and his message. We may look for themes – or at least reasons why these pieces of teaching are put together – but this is possibly no more than minds from another age trying to impose their patterns of thought on what they have received. Luke refuses to be confined in this way, so we are left with a collage of free-standing sayings, some short, some rather longer, but all of them demanding attention in their own right.

Among them there are some of the most striking parables to have come down to us – the parable of the banquet and the reluctant guests (Luke 14:16-25), the prodigal son (Luke 15:11-32), the dishonest steward (Luke 16:1-8), the rich man and the beggar (Luke 16:19-31), and the Pharisee and the publican (Luke 18:9-14). What makes each of these parables a masterpiece is that so much of life is there – they depend on accurate observation at several levels to be so true to life –   yet they speak of things beyond our daily existence and point the way to faith. They speak of God, his ways and his purpose for us, while also holding up to each reader the kind of mirror which penetrates the surface of life. So, the parable of the reluctant guests not only talks with unusual directness about the way people order their lives, but it suggests that their response of indifference to Jesus means that others will have the opportunity to enter into the kingdom. Luke's audience will be quick to understand the good news of this parable – that it is God's will to open the kingdom to them as well; in the black and white world of Jew and Gentile, the Chosen Race and those outside, this is both revolution and revelation. In the Jewish world where everything is judged by the law, to have a God who searches for those who are lost and who welcomes those who return to him stands on its head the usual pattern of thinking of the religious community. For those who live outside the world of legal rectitude this is a magnanimity that offers hope and restoration. The parable of the Pharisee and the publican stands on its head so many of the assumptions of the religious life; it is the generosity of God which confounds the expectations of those who for their moral superiority expect to be heard.

Only the parable of the dishonest steward gives the reader problems of interpretation. The difficulty lies in where the parable ends, and the comments or explanations begin. Does Jesus commend the steward for being dishonest? Was Jesus making a moral point about the right use of money (even the explanation seems rather forced), or was Jesus' point that even this evil man could read the situation he was faced with – how could the religious people of Jesus' day not recognise what God was doing in the person of Jesus? It is this last interpretation which fits best the challenges of Jesus' ministry.

The parable of the dishonest steward brings to an end this long section of teaching. What Luke has managed to accomplish in this passage is to bring balance to his message. Jesus is shown to be a person whose message and actions are at one: his message is that of mercy and hope, compassion and love, regardless of race or religious rectitude; he speaks to his readers of the magnanimity of God which is in complete contrast to the preachers of the day. At the same time, Jesus has by his actions of healing and restoration fulfilled the promises of God as Isaiah set them out. The time has now come to move on, and he takes up the traditional order of things (Luke 18:15) with his account of Jesus' welcome of the children.

The approach of a rich man asking *'Good Teacher, what must I do to win eternal life?'* (Luke 18:18) is a rather shorter version of Mark 10:17-31, just as the prophecy of Jesus' approaching death is both less detailed and less dramatic; the death he must die will be cruel, painful and agonising, but Luke does not dwell on this side of it, either here or in the Passion Narrative itself. Since the journey to Jerusalem began, there has been no note of their progress. Now Jericho is mentioned; it will not be long before Jesus is in the great city once again. Before they can start the long climb which will bring them in sight of the city, two men stand in his way: a blind beggar (Luke does not name him) who calls Jesus 'Son of David' begs to have his sight back – and both his faith and his persistence are rewarded; Zacchaeus finds his life transformed because Jesus notices him and chooses to be his guest. A man who had built his whole life on money – and he had a reputation to match – found in Jesus' recognition of him a freedom money could not give. It was a very public renunciation of his former life – and just as publicly, Jesus hailed the transformation that had taken place: *'Today salvation has come to this house – for this man too is a son of Abraham.'* (Luke 19:9)

The parable which Luke now inserts into the traditional order of things tells us what Luke is thinking: Jesus, the King, is coming to his capital; it is a moment of judgement, not least for those who do not recognise Jesus as their King.

All the elements of Jesus' entry into Jerusalem which both Mark and Matthew include in their descriptions of this event are to be found in Luke's record as well: the colt has not yet been ridden, and so is fit for holy use; Jesus rides as king, and his supporters hail him; their words pick up words from the Psalms, although Luke omits 'Hosanna' – perhaps because he thought his audience would not understand it. But even in this celebratory moment, the Pharisees disapprove – so the event is not unalloyed joy – and Jesus weeps over the city because it is so blind to the real nature of the moment and to who it is that comes. Jesus speaks of the tragedy which must befall the city – Luke's description is chillingly accurate and dramatic – and all because they did not seize the moment when it came. This city, above all, was intended to be a city of peace; it has failed to live up to its calling, and so it is to be a city of conflict and of pain.

Luke's story of Jesus setting the Temple to rights is brief (two verses) – almost as if it is were overwhelmed by Jesus' lament which preceded it. But however short the account, Jesus' action will provoke a response which will have its place in the final drama. In the meantime, Jesus faces questions which suggest that he is being taken very seriously. The first question is about authority – who gave him permission to act as he did? In one sense, they knew the answer: it was not any ecclesiastical body that had sanctioned his actions. For them, all authority is given; they are invested with authority by reason of their rank or position. Their authority comes from the religious structure: there is never any thought that his authority was innate or God-given, so Jesus' riposte takes them by surprise, and they find themselves on the horns of a dilemma of their own making. Luke follows Mark in relating the parable of the evil tenants at this point, and so ensuring that there could be only one interpretation, and heightens the intensity of the ending by adding to the quotation from Psalm 118 with *'Everyone who falls on that stone will be dashed to pieces; anyone on whom it falls will be crushed.'* (Luke 20:18)

Luke does not name the Pharisees as the next group of protagonists, as Mark does; he presents the question of tribute to Caesar as part of a continuing battle. Certainly, whoever questioned Jesus hoped to place him in an impossible position; whichever answer he gave would bring trouble – either from the occupying power or from Jewish loyalists. But Jesus is wise enough to look deeper than the answers offered him, and his answer not only avoids the trap set for him, but invites his questioners to examine themselves about the true nature of their own loyalties and action: *Pay to Caesar what belongs to Caesar, and to God what belongs to God.'*

The Sadduccees fared no better when they tried to catch Jesus out. Luke puts his own touches to the clash, adding greatly to the way Jesus talks of life beyond the grave for those who share in the resurrection – an essential addition for Gentile people who would be less than familiar with the kind of Jewish beliefs which would have stood behind this argument. For much the same reason – 'which is the greatest commandment of all?' is very much a Jewish question – he omits the final question of Mark's sequence, and moves directly to Jesus' challenge about the Messiah and his denunciation of how legal experts used to behave. The material is much the same, but we are not left with the feeling that Jesus has established himself as the supreme authority in interpreting scripture, as we find in Mark.

Chapter 21 follows the tradition we have received in Mark 13. There are considerable variations in details, but every part of Mark's 'little apocalypse' is represented. He speaks of *Jerusalem encircled by armies'* (Luke 21:20), as may well have happened in AD 70, and verses 23 and 24 seem to be describing the lot of a conquered people. Disciples must expect arrest and to experience bitter rejection, even from their own family, because of their faith: *But not a hair of your head shall be lost. By standing firm you will win yourselves life.'* (Luke 21:18 and 19)

The Final Conflict

In all the Gospels the Passion Narrative is essentially the heart of the matter, and it is told with the greatest care and attention to detail. There is no shortage of occasions when Luke tells the story his way, adding material in some places, omitting details which have seemed so important in the other accounts. Even when he follows the traditional pattern, there is hardly a verse which is not changed. This is very much Luke's account.

The first change may well not be very surprising. Luke has already told a story of a woman anointing Jesus (Luke 7:36-38), so it is not included here as well. In doing this Luke destroys the neat introduction we find in Mark and Matthew of the protagonists in the drama which is about to unfold. So too, the Passover meal has a very different feel to it. Variations in texts give us a major headache at this point, and it is beyond the scope of this book to go into the detail of it. It seems that Luke alone presents words over a cup, then the bread is given, followed by another cup. The words which accompany these actions differ from version to version – possibly a sign that someone has smoothed over difficulties in the text by including familiar words from elsewhere. In this longer text, Jesus adds to his brief *This is my body'* the words *'which is given for you; do this as a memorial of me.'* In the same way he took the cup after the meal and said, *'This cup, poured out for you, is the new covenant sealed in my blood.'* In this text, the first cup is not seen as being part of the institution of the Eucharist: it is a moment of dedication – marked by abstinence, as is traditional: Jesus is dedicating himself for the action which will bring in the kingdom. Wine is a drink of celebration; it belongs to the time when the kingdom is a reality, to which Jesus refers in verse 30. Then come the familiar words with the bread and the cup. Would a close companion of Paul really have omitted the words we find in 1 Corinthians 11:23-26?

Logic then drives the action: if Jesus is to die, who will lead them? Hence the dispute, which seems so out of place to us, but if the disciples had never entertained the possibility of Jesus dying, questions of leadership may never have arisen before this moment. Jesus prophesies that Peter will deny him, and Peter responds in typically robust fashion – but Jesus will be proved right as events unfold. Danger is in the air – for all of them, not just for Jesus – and Jesus underlines their need to be ready to face it. Luke's use of Isaiah 53:12, *'He was numbered with transgressors,'* heightens the sense of danger, but also points to the hidden dimension in the whole drama: in what looks to be a human drama the will of God is also to be seen.

They arrive at Gethsemane which is not named by Luke. Twice Jesus tells his disciples to pray that they may be *'spared the test'* – he knows that what lies ahead of him is far more than testing, and his prayer to the Father reflects this. In Luke's description we are shown both Christ's agony and the Father's response – *'sweat was like drops of blood'* and *'an angel from heaven brought him strength'*; in contrast, the disciples slept. The arresting party, if Luke is to be believed, must have been a strange affair: led by Judas, there seem to have been members of the Temple guard, chief priests and elders, and even a serving maid who later recognised Peter. The act of betrayal was a kiss – an act of close personal affection used to bring about arrest, injustice and death, and when violence was on the point of breaking out, it was Jesus' action which stemmed it. At this point, Luke gives us a different order of events. There is no hearing before the assembly until morning – and that was a hurried affair before placing Jesus in front of the Governor. Instead, he tells us of Peter's denial, a sad series of challenges to Peter – all the more difficult to resist because they were seemingly so inconsequential. Luke alone records one moment which seems to capture something of the heart of what was happening: *'The Lord turned and looked at Peter. Peter remembered the Lord's words: "Tonight, before the cock crows you will disown me three times," And he went outside and wept bitterly.'* (Luke 22:62)

Jesus' appearance before the nation's leading experts can hardly be called a trial. As Luke tells it, it is brief, informal and quite unlike any judicial procedure about which such religious and legal experts would have been absolutely scrupulous. Jesus' response to the opening question lays the situation out very clearly: there is complete breakdown. Jesus has a message which has been ridiculed and rejected; they feel they have been undermined and condemned; there is no sympathy, no understanding, no recognition. All they were looking for was grounds for placing Jesus before the Governor on a capital charge. From what Jesus said it was not difficult to concoct a charge which would carry a death penalty. Truth, let alone religious truth, did not come into it.

The trial process in front of Pilate, and then Herod, was no more satisfactory. The accusations against him were serious – but not substantiated; Herod was intrigued, but he cannot be said to have come to any conclusion. Instead, the whole matter descended into a bit of cheap sport before sending him back to Pilate. In describing events in this way, Luke establishes two things: that Jesus was innocent of all the charges against him, and that the drive to have Jesus put to death came entirely from the Jewish leaders and their henchmen. That they were content to have a murderer released completes the picture. Luke's presentation of the trial process does not follow the well-trodden path of Mark and Matthew; it is part of his case that the representatives of the Roman Empire are not responsible for Jesus' death – he was never a threat to them; nor are his followers. In tune with this, there is no making sport of Jesus by the Roman soldiers, and the final pronouncement by the centurion, 'Beyond doubt, this man was innocent,' (Luke 23:47) is the final verdict on the whole event.

Luke brings to his presentation of the crucifixion his own particular insights, all of them illustrated by the different episodes he records. The one thing Luke hardly mentions at all is what must have been at the centre of it all – the crucifixion itself. It is known to have been a cruel, degrading, painful and humiliating manner of execution; none of this appears in Luke. His account brings in elements no other writer uses: Jesus' words to the women of Jerusalem are selfless and moving; he knows very well that the wilful blindness which has led to his death will also bring about terrible consequences for them. Equally, he is aware that the soldiers who inflict such pain on him are 'only doing their job.' They can have no understanding of other dimensions to this all too frequent form of execution. Even his assurance to the thief who hangs with him has a magnanimity which is in complete contrast to such terrible surroundings. It is all part of Luke's message to his readers: here is our Christ, a man of compassion and generosity and understanding, even at this terrible moment.

The note of the darkness is followed by Luke recording that the curtain of the Temple was destroyed. This happens before Jesus' final words: *'Father, into your hands I commit my spirit.'* This is an unexpected sequence, since elsewhere the tearing of the curtain follows Jesus' death. But Luke is determined to allow nothing to take away from the final verdict by the centurion. The burial too is hasty – but not without its reference to the innocence of Jesus. Luke ends his account by noting that the women saw where the body was put, and went home to prepare spices and ointment, so that the rituals of death could be completed when the Sabbath had passed.

In chapter 24 Luke leads his readers through the experience and discovery of Easter. The day begins in very early morning with the women, whom Luke is careful to name – though there were also other women present – going to the tomb to anoint the body of Jesus. There was no expectation of resurrection, indeed no understanding of what resurrection might be. Their only awareness was of loss and death. Gradually they, and the other disciples, are led by experience. It begins with an empty tomb, a puzzling fact for which they have no explanation. Even the explanation of the angels means nothing to the disciples, when the women passed on the message they were given. Luke then treats us to one of the great New Testament stories – the encounter with the risen Christ on the way to Emmaus, and how Jesus *'had made himself known to them in the breaking of the bread.'* It is a great story because it uses all the best features of storytelling – such as Luke rarely displays in the passages he writes. Surely, this is one of the great discoveries unearthed by his research. We are led, as if from inside, from the dismay and disbelief at the death of Jesus, through the dismissal of what they had heard about the tomb being empty, to the point when the stranger they were walking with began an exposition which left them stunned, but not yet believing. It was a simple action – the stranger breaking bread as Jesus used to break it – which produced the moment of recognition and understanding that changed everything. On their return to Jerusalem, they discovered that others had had a similar experience. Finally, there was the shared encounter with the risen Christ, which began in puzzlement and uncertainty. He showed them his hands and his feet; then he ate some fish – a final act of proof – before further words of explanation. *'No ghost has flesh and bones as you can see that I have,'* puts neatly what the Church must have said countless times since to a doubting world.

The power of this presentation is that it does not display empty triumphalism; it begins with doubt; throughout there is puzzlement, even scepticism, as many a person hearing the Easter story for the first time might well have. During all this, the disciples are led by their experience – and this is the kind of evidence to which people respond.

The ending of the Gospel hardly feels like an end. Luke rounds off this part of his two volume project with a great declaration by Jesus, and yet he also makes it clear that this is not an end. Everything points foward; the disciples wait in Jerusalem in hope and expectation - great things are to come but they lie beyond the scope of this book; even the Ascension, final though it is, hardly feels like an end. Jesus' final words combine completion with looking forward to a future in which the apostles will take an active part:

And he said to them, 'This is what I meant by saying, while I was still with you, that everything written about me in the law of Moses and in the Prophets and psalms was bound to be fulfilled. Then he opened their minds to understand the scriptures. 'So you see,' he said, 'that scripture foretells the suffering of the Messiah and his rising from the dead on the third day, and declares that in his name repentance bringing the forgiveness of sins is to be proclaimed to all nations beginning from Jerusalem. You are to be witnesses to it all. I am sending on you the gift promised by my father; wait here in this city until you are armed with power from above.' (Luke 24: 44 to 49)

Our task in this book is to examine and learn more about the Gospels. The Gospel according to St Luke cannot be fully understood without seeing it in partnership with the Acts of the Apostles. In the Gospel, Luke has laid out for a Gentile audience a powerful presentation of the person of Jesus, his actions and his teachings. To believe in this man is to be called to a selfless life, following his example and displaying the same compassion and generosity which is to be found in both Jesus' actions and his teaching. In as many ways as he can, Luke has demonstrated the innocence of Jesus; he has also shared the experience of resurrection in a manner which the most sceptic of listeners will find both challenging and persuasive.

Yet only the first part of Luke's declared intention has been covered; beyond the scope of the Gospel is the task of commending the Christian 'Way,' and those who follow the Jesus he has presented. He plans to show how Christianity came to Rome (although it had certainly arrived there long before Paul). These events too are almost certainly in his mind, even as he wrote the first few lines of his Gospel. In the same way, the opening words of the Acts of the Apostles suggest that all he has written about Jesus is only the beginning of the case he is making. It has been essential that his presentation of Jesus has been seen on the world stage, and that the Good News of Jesus includes and welcomes people beyond the Jewish community. This prepares the reader well for the continuing story which sees the young faith expanding beyond the Jewish homeland.

One serious purpose in putting pen to paper in the first place is to counter false impressions – even accusations – that the followers of Jesus frequently encountered. It is especially in the events surrounding the death of Jesus, the innocence of Jesus, and his compassion for those around him, which speak with great power in a way that distances him and his followers from many of the things said about them. In particular, distance is put between the followers of Jesus and the Jewish religion which the Empire had to make a special case, so difficult were they to accommodate in the secular world of the Roman Empire.

Luke's Gospel is a very human presentation of Jesus, and he has made his case in terms which even those who know little about Jewish things would be able to appreciate. His portrait of Jesus (even if this is not a biography) is of an understanding, compassionate, perceptive and powerful person whose message and actions gave people hope, restored them at every level, and challenged them to take up a way of life that is extraordinarily human, and yet shot through with the presence and power of God. The story Luke tells is utterly human, yet God is everywhere in this record. You cannot encounter Jesus without encountering God – a God who touches people's lives, turns the ways of the world utterly upside down, and offers a life that is credible and attractive. This is the best kind of apologia – commending the Gospel of Christ through experience rather than explanation. Little wonder it has played such an important role in the life of the Church. This is a Gospel for all people – and we are included in its scope.

CHAPTER FIVE

John – A Gospel for all Time

The opening words of the Gospel according to St John have set readers in every generation a formidable challenge. He starts with a cosmic understanding of the story he is about to tell, and so seems to stand on its head the usual way of approaching matters of faith and conviction. For the most part it has been experience which has been the starting-point for the exploration which leads to faith, and reflection and engagement which have led to a deeper understanding of the events which have prompted such a response. John does not give us that luxury. He begins at the point at which many people's journey to faith comes to realisation and fulfilment: that in the life and person of Jesus of Nazareth we see, not just a good man and a wise teacher, but the fullest possible human expression of the fundamental truths of the universe, the very being that gives it coherence and life and completeness. While the other Gospels lead us from the life and ministry, death and resurrection of Jesus to faith and discipleship, and a vision of God's greatness and his salvation, in John's Gospel he begins with the eternal, and presents us with moments in the life of Jesus which are shot through with this deeper dimension, so that in word and deed Jesus gives us windows on the eternal which light up our earthbound human world.

It should be no surprise, then, that this Gospel works in a very different way from the other three. Its methods and content are quite different, and although the life at the centre of this Gospel is recognisably the same life which inspired the Gospels of Matthew, Mark and Luke, from the very first words of this Gospel we are being presented with that life from a very different perspective.

The Prologue

St John's Gospel opens with one of the most famous first lines in all literature: *'In the beginning the Word already was. The Word was in God's presence, and what God was, the Word was.'* (John 1:1)

95

Translations vary, but so brief is this opening sentence that it is difficult to arrive at a satisfactory translation without multiplying words and limiting the scope of the meaning to which this opening points. There are only three primary ideas – beginning, Word and God – and although the temptation to qualify them and describe them more fully is almost overwhelming, attempts are usually clumsy and rob the opening of its all-inclusive nature. The opening sentence does two things: it sets out the scope of what this book is about, and it attracts the interest of any potential reader. Any thinker in the late first or early second century, whether from the Greek or Jewish world, would have been instantly alerted by reference to the '*Word*', and been drawn in to follow the line of thought being introduced. Above all, this opening engages minds that have wrestled with the mysteries of our existence – its origin, its purpose, where it all came from – and sets out something far more fundamental than an explanation: this Gospel begins with a credo which embraces all the philosophies and understandings people have come to, and draws them together into a new and profound expression of the fundamentals of life.

The single term *logos* (word) incorporates all the different shades of meaning which allow this to happen. John does not seek to define his terms; instead, as the Gospel unfolds, we shall see how Jesus expresses the mind and will of God; his Word is command – and so by his Word creation came into being, and recreation is brought about through his death and resurrection. But *logos* also translates as 'reason,' 'principle,' or 'meaning,' and it is through the action of the *logos* that creation has an inner cohesion; he is the One who provides meaning and purpose for everyone he brings into being. This Gospel is about the *logos* in action in all these ways, but there is one difference between the *logos* John presents and all the ways in which others have written and spoken about *logos*: '*So the Word became flesh; he made his home among us, and we saw his glory, such glory as befits the Father's only Son, full of grace and truth.*' (John 1:14)

Through Jesus, the *logos* is experienced in human, tangible form. There is nothing ethereal or unreal about the life that was lived. He ate, he wept, he walked, and died. The record John gives confirms this. But as we watch this life, we are being shown the *logos* at work, expressing the Father's will and disclosing to us the power and purpose of God himself

In the Prologue, other key words are introduced – all with a history in the thinking and philosophies of those who had struggled with the fundamental truths of life. Both '*light*' and '*life*' are words that regularly featured in religious and philosophical thinking, as people tried to express truths they were discovering. But words which in their hands were used symbolically, John now incorporates in tangible form in the 'Word made flesh.' Here is the one who will make possible *'life in all its fullness.'*

'Light' draws some of its meaning from its opposite with which it constantly wrestles – *'darkness'* – and that is part of the drama which will unfold. But there is one more affirmation before this part of the prologue is complete: the conflict between *'light'* and *'darkness'* is ages old, yet for all the power of 'darkness', the *'light shines in the darkness, and the darkness has never mastered it'.* (John 1:5) The word John uses for 'mastered' is a little ambiguous; it can mean 'mastered' or 'overwhelmed,' but it can also mean 'understood.' John wants us to hang on to all these meanings as we reflect on the *'light.'*

The Prologue to this Gospel, however, is rather more than a brief sketch of the theological basis for what follows; with the introduction of John the Baptist, John the theologian becomes specific; at a particular time and through a particular individual the action began – the purpose was for him to be *'a witness to testify to the light'* (John 1:7). The coming of the *logos* is not without paradox: he is coming into a world he was instrumental in bringing into being, and he came to a people who called themselves 'The Chosen People', yet there was no recognition and no response from the very people who might have been expected to recognise him. The opportunity was there for all to grasp – and it remains open to all who come to recognise him – and for all who do, something astonishing is possible: they will be made *'children of God.'* This is the mystery at the heart of what follows.

The Prologue also helps us to understand what is happening in the events which John relates. From the end of chapter 2 to chapter 12 Jesus is involved in countless conversations and controversies; from Nicodemus' visit at night (chapter 3) to the feeding of the five thousand (chapter 6) and the healing of the man born blind (chapter 9), Jesus is met with incredulity, rejection, even attempts to stone him. All this we are prepared for as John writes: *'He came to his own, and his own people would not accept him'* (John 1:11). From chapters 13 to 17, Jesus is with his friends and followers, feeding, teaching, strengthening them for the ordeal that they too are about to go through. They are those who as his followers, *'put their trust in him,'* and to them *'he gave the right to become children of God'* (John 1:12). In this most complex Gospel, the Prologue gives us an insight into what is really happening.

Finally, the Prologue lays out for us the great contrast between the gifts Christ brings with all that has preceded him: *'From his full store we have all received grace upon grace; for the law was given through Moses, but grace and truth came through Jesus Christ. No one has ever seen God; God's only Son, he who is nearest to the Father's heart, has made him known.'* (John 1:16-18)

For this part of his preparation John speaks with a rather more Jewish voice. God's own preparation for the coming of Christ is to be found in the history of the Jewish people. What John now presents takes us beyond preparations to a new reality. The contrast is striking; but in the pages which follow we shall be blessed with a glimpse of the One who is God.

The Witness of John the Baptist

The suddenness of the move from the Prologue to the witness of John the Baptist is a reminder that we are reading a very different kind of Gospel from those we have already examined. However much we might have been tempted to try to use the other Gospels as biographies, that is impossible when studying the Gospel of John. The rapid changes of scene and sequence make it well-nigh impossible to plot a coherent story; more telling is the way John goes about conveying his message. It is not that the miracles of Jesus, the healings and the feeding of the five thousand for instance, are unimportant, but that John's message lies beyond them, in the discussions Jesus has and the confrontations he becomes engaged in.

Perhaps we should not be surprised that the author who opens his Gospel by talking about the Word, should be most careful to present his message through the spoken word which he records. He begins with the spoken word on the lips of John the Baptist and the responses to Jesus spoken by those who first became his disciples. But soon enough conversations with Nicodemus and the Samaritan woman, to name but two, will be the medium through which John conveys his message. And John has his own style, which is not always easy to follow. He does not build neat arguments or give us sequences of propositions which build logically to a conclusion. Reading John is not unlike playing chess with an original and forever surprising companion, who, as the game goes on, continually produces sudden and unexpected moves for which there seem no obvious preparation. As the conversations or debates proceed, John regularly produces statements which carry great authority, but cannot be deduced from what has gone before. At times, it is almost as if he is thinking as he speaks, drawing thoughts and convictions in from every side, whether they have a logical place in the argument or not. It makes for challenging reading – but it also gives us insights and truths we might never have imagined possible.

John's use of language is different from the other Gospels. He uses words and phrases that were widely used in the world of Greek philosophy and religion, as well as everyday life. Some clearly have their roots in the philosophy of Plato; others were extensively used by the Stoics. Knowledge is a key word in this Gospel, as it was for the Gnostics of the first and second century. This does not mean that John was a Platonist or a Stoic or a Gnostic. His use of words and phrases was quite deliberate: through them he was reaching out to a world which would otherwise have been wholly cut off from Christ and his Good News. He spoke their language in order to take them beyond their present understandings and find in Christ the fulfilment of all their hopes and aspirations. Christ is the 'I am' not only for the Jews, but also for the Greek world which was also longing to discover true life and salvation. But we must not think of this Gospel as 'the Greek Gospel;' so much of it springs from Jewish scriptures and the Jewish way of thinking. Both alike are embraced in order to bring both to the fulfilment which Christ makes possible.

John the Baptist is a person set apart. He appeared on the religious scene quite unexpectedly, and his baptism in the River Jordan of those who came to him attracted people from many parts of the community. He also caught the attention of the religious authorities, and their cross-examination of him displays a certain amount of nervousness about what it all meant. Messianic fever was in the air; they needed to have a clear answer, but behind the questions lie religious politics as much as religious enquiry – and that will take centre stage as events come to their climax.

For all that, this is a very different presentation of John the Baptist and his ministry, although many of the elements with which we are familiar from the other Gospels can be found. In very different words we hear echoes of 'I baptise with water; he will baptise you with the Holy Spirit,' and 'I am not worthy to unfasten the strap of his sandal.' 'The Spirit came down like a dove,' and 'after me comes a man who ranks before me.' Most important of all these references to other accounts of John the Baptist is the quotation from Isaiah: *I am a voice crying in the wilderness; "Make straight the way of the Lord".* In every account this is the scriptural authority for his role and ministry. Here it is also used to deflect questions about his messianic credentials. His emphatic 'no' needed that further confirmation – *He readily acknowledged, "I am not the Messiah." "What then? Are you Elijah?" "I am not," he replied. "Are you the Prophet?" "No".'* (John 1:20-21) The chosen quotation from Isaiah carried no messianic connotation for those who were questioning him. Nevertheless, it spoke of the role he had been given, and those who questioned him must have understood that his ministry was a response to God's call.

What is unique to this Gospel is the way John the Baptist describes the purpose of his own ministry, and what he had experienced which pointed to Jesus: his seeing the Spirit descending fulfilled what he had been told, and identified Jesus to be the One who is to come, *'God's Chosen One.'* (John 1:34) Twice, he calls Jesus the *'Lamb of God,'* and it is this witness to Jesus which helps to draw the first disciples to Jesus, and begins the sequence of events in which we are told of their responses to him. As the one who was sent to prepare the people for the coming of the Messiah, it is a surprise that John the Baptist does not use messianic language more extensively. This, however, may be because he understands that the role Jesus is destined to fulfil goes far beyond the range of Jewish expectations. He is to be the cosmic redeemer, fulfilling his role in suffering and dying – much as the Passover Lamb whose blood on the doorpost meant that the angel of death 'passed over' and did not touch the first-born of the house (Exodus 15). One sentence expresses all this: *'There is the Lamb of God,' he said 'who takes away the sin of the world'* (John 1:29). This whole passage is a mixture of high theology and simple story: the significance of John's witness to Jesus is immense; the drawing of the first disciples around him so human and uncomplicated that no one would have thought of inventing it. There will be other moments in the Gospel when we shall see the same combination. It is a reminder that this Gospel has within it several different kinds of material, each of which communicates at its own level.

If this is rather a heady mixture, John does give us some help. The author separates out the different stages by using notes of time. Three times we hear the phrase *'on the next day,'* and on each occasion the story has moved on. If John the Baptist did not use a great deal of messianic language, the terms in which Andrew and Philip responded to Jesus fully make up for it. All are changed by their encounter with Jesus, and the presentation of Jesus can now move on to the next stage.

Signs and Symbols in Action

The public ministry of Jesus has not yet started. He goes as a guest to a wedding – perhaps he was a friend of the family – and not unsurprisingly Mary, his mother, was also there. The exchange between them, when the observant Mary noticed a catering crisis looming, is often misunderstood. Some translations make Jesus sound as if he was trying to assert his independence rather more than brusquely! *'That is no concern of mine'* (John 2:4) is quite gentle by comparison with some translations. But the home links had not yet been broken, and following the wedding feast John tells of Jesus going to Capernaum with his mother and his brothers. *'My hour has not yet come'* – the time for public action, doing the Father's will and speaking and acting in his name is still in the future. Yet in deference to his mother he gives orders to the servants, and social disaster is averted. But however much he tried to remain hidden, his disciples knew; the event opened their eyes, and their understanding of Jesus is deepened. John calls this a sign – an action which points beyond itself to the true identity of Jesus – and so we are introduced to one of John's ways of presenting Jesus which we will meet again as the Gospel continues.

Time and place are important in any drama, and in the end it will be at Jerusalem that the crucial action will happen. Jerusalem, and in particular the Temple, is the centre of everything to do with the faith, and after a short delay it is to Jerusalem Jesus goes for the first of his great public actions. The other Gospels place their account of Jesus' action in the Temple late on in his ministry; John begins Jesus' public ministry with his action of clearing the Temple. In the other Gospels, Jesus receives a tumultuous welcome; John tells of him going up to Jerusalem without any accompanying crowds. (The welcome is later and rather different in this gospel.) They speak of him quoting the prophets and roundly condemning the blind commercialism of the Temple trade; in John his words are more prohibition than outraged condemnation. His action (in the tradition of so many prophetic actions in past generations) is inevitably seen as a challenge to the established order. The authorities responded as authorities always do; they ask for a sign – some proof of suitable authority to act in this way – but when Jesus answers them they cannot have been any the wiser. (What an absurd suggestion! Rebuild the Temple in three days? It has already taken forty-six years to build!) Only much later could any kind of meaning be attached to Jesus' words – and this the author supplies, as any good editor would. But this is more than a helpful footnote: the significance of Jesus' words is central to the unfolding of the Gospel; by dying and rising Jesus himself becomes the focus of God's presence among his people, replacing the Temple.

There is more to Jesus' stay in Jerusalem than his action in the Temple. He is attracting attention with other things he is doing. John calls them 'signs' and people are beginning to respond to him, although Jesus is wise enough not to set much store by what people are saying.

Nicodemus

Among those who responded to Jesus was Nicodemus. Apart from this conversation (at night, which may have been to avoid being seen talking to this controversial firebrand), we only hear of Nicodemus when the arguments were raging (John 7:50) and at the burial of Jesus. From what we are told, it is difficult to know Nicodemus' rank or position on the Council of the Jews, but we are intended to understand that he was a considerable person; at one point Jesus calls him 'a teacher in Israel.' (John 3:10) If we hope to be able to follow the conversation as if we were in the room with them, we shall be disappointed. John has his own ways, and they are particularly unusual.

Tracing the to and fro of the communication is instructive, and it will help us to understand future conversations – not least the Samaritan woman in chapter 4 and the healing of the man at the Pool of Bethesda in chapter 5.

Nicodemus opens with generous words (they are not flattering; he was genuinely puzzled, and does not want to put questions to Jesus just to catch him out). *'We know that you are a teacher sent by God: no one could perform these signs of yours unless God were with him.'* Jesus' reply is utterly surprising: *'In very truth I tell you, no one can see the kingdom of God unless he has been born again.'* His words do not naturally follow from what Nicodemus said. A great deal has been left unspoken, and Jesus has introduced two new ideas – *'kingdom of God,'* and *'born again.' 'Kingdom of God'* will have had some meaning for Nicodemus – but very probably he thought of a literal kingdom, like the kingdom of which David was king – so it is no surprise that in his reply he treats being *'born again'* literally too. There is no meeting of minds, and the gap only gets wider.

We are bound to ask why the Gospel writer wants to record this breakdown of understanding (at least on Nicodemus' part), and the clue is in the terms Jesus uses. We find phrases like *'born again,'* and *'born from water and spirit'* (John 3:5) and *'Flesh can give birth only to flesh; it is spirit that gives birth to spirit'* (John 3:6). To the Christian community Jesus' words point unmistakably to baptism, and Jesus is contrasting it to circumcision *('flesh')*. This is a battleground between Jew and Christian as to who inherits God's promises – enters his kingdom – and the life he gives.

Two other elements of this passage are important if we are to understand its message, and what it tells us about this Gospel and the context in which it was created. Jesus says, 'we speak of what we know;' and *'No one has gone up into heaven except the one who came down from heaven, the Son of Man who is in heaven'* (John 3:13). If the question is asked, 'How do you know?' the answer lies in the fact that we are seeing at work the logos that came from heaven, and can draw on what he knows directly from the Father. John can thus end this conversation not only with an interpretation of the death of Jesus on the Cross, but a glorious statement of the purpose of God in the coming of Jesus (John 3:16-17): *'God so loved the world that he gave his only Son, that everyone who has faith in him may not perish but have eternal life. It was not to judge the world that God sent his Son into the world, but that through him the world might be saved.'*

Behind the glorious words lies controversy and profound differences between the Jewish faith and the faith which sprang from the life and experience of Jesus. This is one of the underlying currents of this Gospel. In chapter 3, the differences are quite gently expressed; in later chapters they become more abrasive and hostile. This is inevitable: not only did the Jewish religious authorities take the initiative in bringing about the death of Jesus, but the growth of the Church set it apart from the Jewish faith. John's Gospel came into existence when the feuding had already been going for decades and the two sides had established their positions at some depth. What we read now needed considerable time to mature; St John's Gospel is not an early response to the situation which grew and changed as the years went by. Controversy is part of the background and it has played its part in shaping the Gospel.

The Samaritan Woman

The conversation with the Samaritan woman (John 4:8-42) is another moment when there is no meeting of minds. A chance encounter it may have been, but there are some features of the conversation we are already familiar with.

To collect water in the middle of the day is hardly the best time, but this woman with a past has her reasons: she will meet no one, and there will be no opportunity for tongues to wag. To find a Jew actually speaking to her must have been a shock. Every prejudice, every taboo is broken by Jesus asking for a drink of water. It is not long, however, before they are talking on very different levels: the woman is practical, and points out that Jesus does not have a bucket (John notes that Jews and Samaritans do not share vessels – and much else); Jesus talks of *'living water.'* And whoever drinks it *'will never again be thirsty.'* That sounds very attractive to her; she will never have to come all the way to the well in the heat of the day. Drinking water – *'living water'* – there is no meeting of minds, but John gets his teaching across-that Jesus, and Jesus alone, is the source of an inner strength and spirit that fills the soul and sustains it in all the challenges of life (John 4:13-14).

The conversation moves on, and Jesus confronts her in a way she could not have expected. At this she realises that the man in front of her is no ordinary person, and puts to him the vexed question on which Jews and Samaritans disagree. Jesus' answer goes much further than the two possibilities the woman had suggested: *'God is spirit, and those who worship him must worship in spirit and in truth'* (John 4:24). Jesus' answer looks beyond the squabble between Jews and Samaritans, and speaks of the worship called for from people of every nation – a fundamental principle for people of faith wherever they come from (he has his very cosmopolitan audience in mind).

With the arrival of the disciples who had gone into town to buy provisions, the story moves on. The woman had also gone into town to spread the word about the man she had met at the well. The disciples urge Jesus to eat, but Jesus replies, using meat and drink figuratively, *'For me it is meat and drink to do the will of him who sent me until I have finished his work.'* Here is the driving passion of his life which the disciples have yet to discover.

Meanwhile the townspeople set out to see for themselves the man about whom the woman had spoken, and the sight of the people approaching draws another picture from Jesus – harvest – the time of fulfilment and reward, when all hope is realised as the crop is gathered in. And this will be a surprising harvest indeed – people who are Samaritans coming to faith in Christ not only through the words of the woman but from their own experience as well. Experience is so often the touchstone which leads to faith: in their case, hearsay has turned to discovery, and discovery becomes conviction and faith. It is a journey which Jesus' followers make and they must be good at helping others to make that same journey.

Jesus travels north from Samaria to Galilee. The welcome he receives contrasts with his reception in Jerusalem, and prompts the comment that *'a prophet is without honour in his own country'* (John 4:44). This seems to stand on its head what we have read in the other Gospels; the same saying was applied to his reception in Nazareth. More likely, it reflects the fact that in this Gospel most of the important action is centred in Jerusalem, and for John that must be the place that counts. The story is not unlike one told by Matthew and Luke. What stands out is the faith of the officer in the royal service who approached Jesus (John 4:46) – strong enough to do what Jesus said without any proof, and it is those who trust Jesus as the officer did who receive his healing and have their faith deepened.

Healing and the Sabbath

No sooner has Jesus arrived in Galilee than he is once again in Jerusalem. There is no attempt to make a connected story; event follows event, but the heart of each story is in the conversations or confrontations which follow the action. The healing of the man at Bethesda takes place on a Sabbath, but the sight of a man carrying his own mattress proved too much for the religious people, and the argument begins. Carrying his mattress was work – forbidden on the Sabbath. But Jesus, in healing the man, said, *'Stand up, take your bed and walk.'* A moment's reflection on this act of healing would show that standing (when the man had been bedridden), taking up his bed and walking, is part of the healing process – rediscovering strength and what he is now capable of after Jesus' word of command. How else could the man have known? How else could he be free of the prison of many years of immobility? But none of these things were understood by the religious law-keepers. The challenge Jesus lays down is to recognise the true nature of his action, and to acknowledge that what he had done was not to infringe God's will, but to do it. But this is far too subtle for his critics; they can only see the law being broken, and that is enough to prove Jesus to be against the law.

The argument goes further: healing is God's work, not the work of the devil. This healing is of God, and, as Jesus puts it, *'My Father continues to work, and I must work too'* (John 5:17). The charge goes deeper than simply breaking the law: they charge him with making himself equal with God - so at least they have understood the implications of Jesus' actions – and those who have read the Prologue are seeing the truth laid out there being confirmed in what Jesus does – but the Jews have withheld their belief and their welcome of the healing, even though it is an action of mercy and compassion. Those who condemn Jesus in this way judge themselves. They have evidence enough to believe; John the Baptist has made his witness to Jesus; the nature of the action, which displays the love and compassion of the Father, carries its own message; Jesus too affirms that he is doing the Father's will. All point in the same direction, if they will but respond to the evidence in front of them.

The paragraphs at the end of chapter 5 are particularly intense. It is difficult to present an ordered exposition, because the context in which John is speaking is not stated. The original incident of healing the man on the Sabbath is left behind, and it is clear that John is making a response to some form of challenge – possibly one faced by the Christian community in John's own day. But perhaps the greatest difficulty is the style in which the whole encounter is carried out. What began with an exchange of charge and response has become a monologue, and the focus of the monologue changes rapidly from sentence to sentence. John's presentation has moved from debating a particular point to a fluid analysis of the disbelief and rejection of his opponents. 'His' is ambiguous, necessarily, because although the words are put in Jesus' mouth, the reality may be that the confrontation which powers this analysis may well be between those who reject the Church's evidence and those who are speaking to defend it. What we read from John 5:31 onwards feels less and less like a reported event, and more and more like a current argument which has real urgency on the part of the person who is presenting it.

The Christian Church has always faced the challenge, 'Where is the evidence?' By way of answer, it has never been enough to say 'Jesus said so,' or 'It is in the Bible.' That will be part of the answer Christians give, but part of the answer must also be the nature of the action (or saying) – does it heal or make whole (or speak a truth) – is it of God – or does it destroy, distort (present a false claim), and diminish those who are touched by it? Those who are engaged in confrontations of this kind are always fighting on two fronts – presenting what they believe to be true, and highlighting the ways in which those who oppose them are working on a false and destructive basis. It could not be clearer that John's presentation of Jesus follows this pattern, especially in these central chapters, and we must expect that as the Gospel unfolds we shall again find Jesus in monologue mode, facing challenges that are as much at home in the life of the Church as they are within the life and ministry of Christ.

Bread on Earth and Bread of Heaven

Chapter 6 begins with another sudden change of scene. From Jerusalem we are whisked to the Sea of Galilee with hardly any attempt to make a link of any kind. This time, however, John records two events with which we are familiar from the other Gospels. He tells the story of the feeding of the five thousand and the walking on the water in his own way, and once again an event provides the foundation for differences between Jesus and others which becomes confrontational, as we have almost come to expect. But in this case John separates the actions from the teaching, choosing to place the confrontation and the teaching on the following day, when the people have managed to catch up with Jesus at Capernaum.

Two observations prepare for the feeding: *'a large crowd of people followed him because they had seen the signs he performed in healing the sick.'* John calls Jesus' acts of healing 'signs' and this is a word which will become important as the chapter progresses. John also tells us that the event fell just before the feast of Passover. He is not given to passing on unnecessary bits of information, so we must expect his understanding of what he is recording to be seen in the light of the festival. Two great moments from Israel's past are in John's mind as he describes the feeding: the great escape from Egypt after Passover, and the feeding of the people in the wilderness with manna. It is the response of the people afterwards which sets his account apart from the others: *'When the people saw the sign Jesus had performed,'* introduces a new dimension. Signs are important because they point beyond themselves, but signs are ambiguous, and the people begin to put a very different (and dangerous) interpretation on what they had experienced. When the time comes, Jesus shows us that he will be a very different kind of king from what the people had in mind.

Jesus reads the situation and is nowhere to be seen, so the disciples set out for Capernaum without him. They had gone some distance when they saw Jesus walking on the sea towards them. They were terrified, but Jesus spoke to them, and they took him on board and the crossing was completed. This astonishing moment passes entirely without comment, but it is very much part of what is being presented. Perhaps for John there was no need to elaborate on this extraordinary event; it was all part of the reference back to the crossing of the Red Sea and the feeding of the people in the wilderness and the Passover which were for all Jews essential parts of their spiritual heritage.

It was not until the next day that the people caught up with Jesus, but Jesus was waiting for them: *'In very truth I tell you, it was not because you saw signs that you have come looking for me, but because you ate the bread and your hunger was satisfied. You should work, not for this perishable food, but for the food that lasts, the food of eternal life.'* (John 6:26-27)

These words establish the theme that will be pursued, but it also is the point when we see the division beginning between Jesus and the people. Astonishingly, they ask for a sign – and quote Moses as their example (although Jesus corrects them; it was God who gave the people manna) – yet what they had experienced was a powerful sign of who Jesus is and what he gives, if they had but understood his action. Just as the Father fed his people in the wilderness, so the Son feeds the people in a deserted place. While they were still thinking about bread for the body, Jesus encapsulates the real significance of his presence: *'I am the bread of life. Whoever comes to me will never be hungry, and whoever believes in me will never be thirsty'* (John 6:35). Jesus gives a sustenance which is unfailing and eternal. To the faithful, he is the one through whom they have strength to live, hope to live for, truth to live by. The believer is given full life and eternal life beyond.

The controversy deepens, because it is now centred on who Jesus is: (*'We know his father and mother. How can he say, "I have come down from heaven"?'*) From the Prologue onwards, this Gospel has affirmed that Christ is only to be understood fully when seen as the Word, at one with the Father, and giving eternal life to those who believe. The people have been told the truth, but it is beyond their comprehension, and when he says *'My flesh is real food; my blood is real drink'*, the breakdown is complete. The vivid language of this passage, which proved so difficult for some, has a purpose beyond the controversy of Jesus' day and the people he was speaking to. John has a wider audience in mind. Among them are those who are used to the mystery religions of his time, in some of which were practised sacred meals with the aim of conferring eternal life. John speaks of Jesus in their language in order to tell them that it is in Christ that their practice and aspirations find their true fulfilment. John is aware of the shock his words will cause, but his answer is to be found on the lips of Peter: *'Lord, to whom shall we go? Your words are words of eternal life'* (John 6:68).

We have travelled a long way in the course of this chapter. What began with the sign of a miraculous feeding, a story which had strong echoes of Israel being fed in the wilderness, and which leads to the proclamation of Jesus as *'the Bread of Life,'* a particular action, spectacular in itself, gives rise to an eternal affirmation. While bread is at the heart of the story, the proclamation speaks of Jesus on an entirely different level. John moves beyond the sustenance of life to present Christ as the source of eternal life to those who believe. Christians will quickly understand this teaching in terms of the Eucharist – but the Eucharist is itself a foretaste of the great banquet which will be the mark of the kingdom to come. We should note that John puts his Eucharistic teaching here, and so does not need to mention Jesus' action and words over the bread and the wine when he comes to the Last Supper.

Conflict Deepens

The next two chapters are taken together to help us see the growing tensions which surround Jesus. There is already a sense that Jesus is facing an increasing tide of opposition, but this should not surprise us: from chapter 3 onwards there has almost been a twin-track theme – Jesus disclosing his true identity being met by a corresponding disbelief (even rejection) on the part of those he encounters. But we have been prepared for this. The Prologue says, *'He came to his own, and his own people would not accept him'* (John 1:11). Now, what began in such a gentle fashion in conversation with Nicodemus becomes the rejection of which the Prologue spoke

Most of the action in this Gospel happens at Jerusalem; Jesus' time in Galilee provides the foil-yet even there faith and doubt are side by side. Even members of his own family seem sceptical about him and he is careful to keep his own counsel. His absence at the beginning of the festival enables John to sketch out the undercurrents of hostility, even fear, which were in full flow among those attending the festival. Jesus makes his entrance in his own time, and soon enough we find him teaching in the Temple. These comments about him begin a series of skirmishes. 'How can an unqualified man show such understanding in what he says?' Both horns of their dilemma are true: Jesus' teaching carries an authority and depth that has attracted their recognition, but as for qualifications – he has neither experience nor letters after his name to explain how he has come to such depth. Jesus has his own explanation: he points beyond himself to the true origin of his message: *'My teaching is not my own but his who sent me'* (John 7:16). The world is full of people who have their own opinions, and with that, all too often, goes a certain self-confidence if not arrogance. Jesus is not promoting his own message and so is free from the pitfalls of such self-promotion. He has come to do the will of God, to speak his truth and make his own witness to the will and purpose of God. This is what sets him apart.

The conflict between Jesus and the Jews (often shorthand for the religious authorities) deepens. Jesus knows that he is in real danger – not least because he healed a man on the Sabbath which was perceived as breaking the law. Jesus points out that to kill (which is what they want to do) is also to break the law, and he widens the conflict by raising the question about what happens when requirements of the law conflict. This is bound to happen, and when it does there must be a way of deciding which requirement takes precedence. Jesus' answer is that it must be the nature of the action, rather than the letter of the law, which must guide what judgements are made.

Speculation is never easy to contain, and the speculation around Jesus was made all the more potent by the hopes and expectations of a Messiah to come. But rumour and gossip are rarely well-founded; often the wrong emphasis is given to what little is known. Jesus challenges this: *'I have not come of my own accord; I was sent by one who is true, and him you do not know.'* (John 7:28) Jesus seems to be speaking in riddles; in fact he is laying open to those who listen the truth about himself. This means that he is not subject to the limitations which his critics and opponents are: *'Where I am you cannot come'* (John 7:34).

The final challenge of this chapter is Jesus' call, *'If anyone is thirsty, let him come to me and drink'* (John 7:37). It is not in the traditions, nor even in the Temple, that people will find the refreshment of spirit which will enable them to live. From now on Jesus must replace the things of the past as the source of strength and inspiration for living. This was a challenge to the whole framework of the Jewish religion. The brief editorial John gives rather intrudes on the flow of the story, but he feels the need to give some explanation. He points forward to the life of the Church and the gift of the Spirit which is to come. The speculation with which the chapter ends only underlines the inability of the Jews to understand who was in front of them, and the arguments between them – among whom was Nicodemus who had visited Jesus at night (chapter 3) – suggest enormous confusion, in part recognition that Jesus represents something that is 'from beyond,' in part a determination to judge by the strictest interpretation of scripture.

At this point, some manuscripts tell a dramatic story of judgement. There is no common mind as to whether it belongs here or not, but no other setting in John offers itself. In the story Jesus is invited to condemn a woman caught in adultery – it would seem that the facts of the case are not in doubt. Death by stoning is the punishment the law prescribes. The way the story is framed, it is not only the woman but also Jesus who is being judged. (Did he hold to the law? Was he soft on sin? Would he suggest something else, and so stand against the law?) Jesus' action, first in stooping to write in the dust (and in doing so making no eye-contact with anyone, accused or accusers) and then saying when pressed, *'Let whichever of you is free from sin throw the first stone'* (John 8:7) places the burden of judgement back on the accusers. Gradually, everyone leaves, and Jesus' final words, *'Go; do not sin again'* closes the matter and resolves a difficult confrontation.

The manuscripts which do not print this story begin chapter 8 with another dramatic pronouncement by Jesus: *'I am the light of the world. No follower of mine shall walk in darkness; he shall have the light of life'* (John 8:12). We might have expected Jesus to lead up to such a statement, but this is the beginning of a confrontation which ends in another assertion, and complete rejection by those who were arguing with him: *"'before Abraham was born, I am." They took up stones to throw at him, but he was not to be seen, and he left the Temple'* (John 8:59). Once again, the Prologue provides the essential commentary: John is laying before us another facet of Jesus' true identity, and the reference to light and darkness reminds us of the themes of the Prologue which speak of the true nature of the 'Word'. Jesus can only say these things about himself because he is the 'Word', and his relationship with the Father is the relationship outlined in the Prologue. The readers of the Gospel already have the clue that makes sense of what Jesus is saying. It helps them to understand how Jesus can possibly say what he does about himself. Establishing the truth of his words is no longer a problem when this background is taken into account. But the Jews have not understood because they have not perceived who Jesus is. Their tests and proofs have not brought them to the truth, and so they argue with Jesus and reject his assertions. That, perhaps, is to put it rather politely; they say of Jesus, *'Are we not right in saying that you are a Samaritan, and that you are possessed?'* (John 8:48) But Jesus has been just as blunt about them.

The great series of confrontations is not quite over, but this is the point at which the breakdown is complete. There has been neither meeting of minds nor recognition, despite the signs Jesus has performed and the teaching he has given. What we were told in the Prologue – *'He came to his own, and his own people would not accept him.'* (John 1:11) – has been laid out for us as the Gospel has unfolded. It has been an uncomfortable journey. It is only with faith that the truth John is presenting about Jesus can be perceived, and John notes from time to time that some do believe, even when there is so much rejection. The turning point of the Gospel, however, is still to come.

Chapter 9 begins with the giving of sight to a man who was born blind. It almost goes without saying that it was a Sabbath when Jesus *'made the paste and opened his eyes'* (John 9:14), so inevitably an argument follows: how can Jesus be good and do the work of God when he breaks the law? It only becomes clear at the very end of the chapter that this healing speaks on at least two levels – the healing itself, and the figurative use of giving 'sight' to those who do not 'see.' Those whose job it was to 'see' had proved themselves to be utterly blind; they had judged themselves by their response to Jesus.

Chapter 10 begins with an abrupt change of subject. Some have tried to suggest a link between the failure of religious authorities to recognise Jesus or to offer the appropriate care to those they lead and the theme of 'shepherding', but this is rather forced and obscures the first picture we are given. Shepherding, and the care of the sheep, is a new theme, and Jesus makes more than one approach in order to communicate the full extent of the teaching he wants to share. Other gospels would have used parables, but John does not do parables. His preferred manner of teaching is through the 'I am' sayings, and that is where the chapter is leading us. In this short passage of twenty-one verses, John gives us two 'I am' sayings: *I am the door'* (10:9) (of the sheepfold), and *'I am the good shepherd'* (10:14). They have a common theme but different messages. Both are declarations, disclosing something about Jesus which is to be trusted and to which his readers should respond. The first describes Jesus as a gatekeeper. His task was to keep secure the sheep which were in the enclosure; he would know who had sheep there and would only let those who owned the sheep take them out. The better known picture of Jesus is as the good shepherd. In the Middle East, shepherds lead their sheep, each often making his own distinctive call so that the sheep can follow him; he leads them from the enclosure to the pastures; he is responsible for their safety, and that they are properly fed.

The thrust of Jesus' teaching at each level contrasts him with those who have claimed the right to be heard and followed. He is genuine; they are bogus. He is recognised to be true; they cheat. He guides and leads and brings to pasture; they neither feed the sheep nor protect them from the dangers that threaten them. Jesus comes to give life – *'in all its fullness;'* the fraudulent shepherds behave like thieves who only come *'to steal, kill and destroy.'* Yet the very subject of the shepherd has another dimension altogether: God himself is not only the Father of Israel; he is also the Shepherd of Israel. The Psalms, especially Psalm 23, speak of God as the Shepherd of his people. This is now the role Jesus lives out, and we can see that he is genuine because he gives his life for the sheep. From a picture which draws on the Old Testament to speak of the relationship between God and his people, John speaks of the relationship between Jesus and those who believe in him. John effortlessly goes beyond the comparisons between Jesus and his contemporaries, to reflect on the meaning of the death of Jesus. In dying and rising, Jesus goes ahead of those who have faith in him. Like the Good Shepherd he is, he leads, not only to make the way through death to life safe for those who follow him, but each one he knows and calls and feeds and keeps safe. John goes out of his way to emphasise the important nature of his death; to the casual spectator, Jesus appears to be the victim: yet Jesus says: *'I lay down my life, to receive it back again. No one takes it away from me; I am laying it down of my own free will. I have the right to lay it down, and I have the right to receive it back again.'* (John 10:17-18)

The theme of shepherd and sheep is continued into the next episode, although that seems to have been on an entirely different occasion – but only to underline that those who oppose him are not members of his flock. When Jesus emphasises his unity with the Father, once again the Jews begin to pick up stones, but he challenges them, quoting scripture and asking why they should stone him when his actions are 'of God.' Danger hangs in the air, and Jesus retreats beyond the Jordan; even there people come to him.

Lazarus and Resurrection

The story of the raising of Lazarus plays a critical part in the unfolding of John's Gospel. As a story it also has to carry so much information, so many theological points which John wants to include. He painstakingly sets it all out so that we, as readers, will pick up every nuance of the account we are given. This is, in part, because of the extraordinary nature of the story; in part, it is also because this story moves events towards the final conflict. From the moment that Lazarus was raised from the dead, Jesus was seen as a threat by those who were in positions of power – very dangerous people to antagonise, more dangerous even than those who took offence at what he was saying and threatened to stone him. We are given a clue as to the importance of the story when Jesus says, early on, *'This illness is not to end in death; through it God's glory is to be revealed and the Son of God glorified.'* (John 11:4)

Few stories illustrate better than this the bonds of love and friendship which existed between Jesus and his closest followers. At the death of Lazarus he wept, and shared the natural sorrow which those close to Lazarus felt. The trust which clearly existed between Jesus and the two sisters is an essential part of the story, and part of his humanity which has rarely been so openly displayed in this Gospel. The raising of Lazarus, when we come to it, is dramatic, but John points us to several different elements of the moment. Martha's concern is practical (as we might expect): *'Sir, by now there will be a stench.'* Jesus prays out loud so that those who witness the event can know that both the Father and the Son unite in this action – confirmation of what he has been trying to teach people throughout his ministry (John 11:42). The final commands have a ring of authority about them: *'Lazarus, come out.'* and *'Loose him; let him go.'* John wants us to see that Jesus' action in raising Lazarus is a foretaste of the resurrection he offers to all who believe in him.

What is done by Jesus among his friends at Bethany is not kept among friends; first-hand accounts of what happened fed the rumour-mill of Jerusalem. Some of those who witnessed it came from Jerusalem; others knew people who were there. The impact of Jesus raising Lazarus to life threatened to upset the delicate balance which the leading Jews had worked out with the Romans. For them, it was not questions of theological truth or the activity of God which were central to their response; it was questions of power, preserving the status quo, which preoccupied them, and it was this which drove the authorities towards the final action.

John is careful, however, to show the reader more. We are reminded of the orthodox belief about life after death (John 11:24), but we are only reminded of it in order that we can see that the truth about Jesus demands that we go further, both in our own beliefs about resurrection and in seeing that it is through Jesus that resurrection is held out to us by God. Once again there are 'I am' sayings which encapsulate his teaching: *'I am the resurrection and the life. Whoever has faith in me shall live, even though he dies; and no one who lives and has faith in me shall ever die.'* (John 11:25-26) John uses this remarkable event to speak, not just of the bringing back to life of Lazarus, but of the hope that everyone can have if they come to faith in Jesus. Resurrection and eternal life were the goals of so many sects and religions throughout the ancient world. Jesus goes further than all of them in offering a hope which is tangible and in which believers can be confident. The importance of this chapter, therefore, is not only in the way it moves the drama of the Gospel on towards its climax, it also offers a faith and a hope that are grounded in Jesus, who he is and what he has done. This is what John's Gospel has to say to his contemporary world, but he speaks to every generation with a truth which addresses all our needs. Mortal humanity searches above all for the immortal; human life is forever searching for the eternal. In Jesus we are offered the life for which all peoples have been searching.

Caiaphas' prophetic words, *'it is more to your interest that one man should die for the people, than that the whole nation should be destroyed'* (John 11:50) point us forward to the Passover and the events which will complete all that Jesus came to do. It is no surprise, then, that John does not take us back into another controversy, but moves the story forward in a pattern of events not unlike the sequence of events with which we are familiar from Mark and Matthew. Jesus is at Bethany – but at the house of Mary, Martha and Lazarus, not Simon the leper (Mark 14:3); it is Mary who anoints Jesus' feet – not an unnamed woman who poured the ointment over Jesus' head – and it is at this point that Judas begins to show his real colours. Then comes John's equivalent of Jesus' triumphal entry into Jerusalem (Mark 11, Luke 19 and Matthew 21), but the dynamics of the moment are entirely different. It was people coming from Jerusalem who formed the crowd which hailed Jesus as *'king of Israel'* (John 12:13), the raising of Lazarus being the spark which lit up their support.

All this is in stark contrast to Jesus' reception hitherto, and the change seems to be complete when some Greeks ask to meet Jesus. At this, the whole atmosphere of the Gospel changes, and although there is one more short moment of conflict, the entire direction of the Gospel is altered. It is no accident that this is the moment of change. Since chapter 2, Jesus has been giving the Jews the opportunity to recognise in him the fulfilment of all God's promises. At every turn his witness to God and the purpose of God has been rejected. Now someone is asking to meet him; more importantly they are Greeks, the people who represent the wider world and the search for truth.

The moment is marked in several different ways, all of them underlining the importance of the moment: Jesus' response, *'The hour has come for the Son of Man to be glorified'* is for the first time in the present tense. Up to this point, whenever Jesus has talked of his 'hour' it has always been in the future. Now he faces up to the events which will most fully display the truth about him: he is to fulfil his destiny (and the task placed upon him by the Father). He knows he is to die, and the picture he uses sets out what lies ahead very clearly: *'unless a grain of wheat falls into the ground and dies, it remains that and nothing more; but if it dies, it bears a rich harvest. Whoever loves himself is lost, but he who hates himself in this world will be kept safe for eternal life.'* (John 12:24-25)
The necessity of dying is striking: that is the only way he will be fulfilled. But the outcome is more than simply fulfilling his destiny: Jesus talks of a rich harvest which could not otherwise have been achieved. Equally importantly, John tells of Jesus using similar phrases to those recorded by Mark in his great challenge to *'anyone who wants to be a follower of mine'* (Mark 8:35). The voice from heaven – heard by some as thunder – and a final response by Jesus completes this pivotal moment. The argument that follows should not be allowed to cloud the picture we are given: this is the moment when John finally points his readers towards the Cross.

The Last Supper

John's account of the Last Supper is radically different from the record to be found in the other Gospels. They focus on Jesus' revelation that one of them is to betray him, and on his taking bread and wine, and through them interpreting his death and establishing a new Passover. That is not possible for John who begins his account of the Last Supper by clearly stating that *'It was before the Passover festival.'* (John 13:1) By contrast, John's introduction to the meal goes beyond the surface event, and allows us to understand what he had in mind as he brings us to this moment; another essential part of the background is Judas' private intentions. In its own way, it is a prologue to the climax of the Gospel, every bit as essential to understanding the events to be set out as was the Prologue in chapter 1. John gives us the theological perspective from which he wants us to respond to the unfolding story. Jesus *'must leave this world and go to the Father,'* although the death he is to die displays no outward sign of this; he *'had come from God and was going back to God,'* those who had followed the working out of the Gospel from the beginning would have been prepared for this. When almost everything from his arrest onwards seems to be done to him, John says that Jesus is *'well aware that the Father had entrusted everything to him,'* and asks us to be alert to the way at his arrest, at his trial before Pilate, even in his final words he is the person who is very much in charge.

The first act of love – *'He had always loved his own who were in the world, and he loved them to the end'* (John 13:1) – was to wash the disciples' feet. Such a menial task was for slaves and slaves alone, but the action of Jesus in taking a towel and washing their feet proved almost too much for them – Peter especially. Unthinkable! But when Jesus explained its real significance, being at one with him, nothing could have been more important. But this action, standing as it does at the very beginning of the movement towards the Cross, describes the nature and purpose of all that follows. It is to cleanse and wash away all the failure and sin of the human race that his greatest act of love (in giving himself on the Cross) is undertaken. And there is sin and failure to come: in the next few hours Peter will deny Jesus three times, and Judas will betray him. Even his closest friends and followers will need the cleansing and the forgiveness which the Cross will bring about. Jesus gives a further interpretation to his action: *'I have set you an example: you are to do as I have done for you.'* (John 13:15) Later, Jesus rephrases and extends this: *'I give you a new commandment: love one another; as I have loved you, so you are to love one another.'* (John 13:34)

The second act of love is a surprising one: he gives a sop to Judas. Such an action is a sign of particular closeness and favour. Judas needs to know that whatever he has planned – and however evil it is – Jesus does not exclude him from the love he has shown to all the disciples. Whatever he decides to do is done in the full knowledge of Jesus' love for him. So when Judas responds by leaving, the nature of the moment is captured by the simple words, *'It was night.'*

With Judas leaving, the final action comes a step closer, and Jesus turns his attention to the needs of the disciples, because they too have an ordeal to come. His word to them is to 'trust' – *'Trust in God always; trust also in me.'* (John

14:1) When they cannot understand what is happening, and when what they are caught up in is the very opposite of what they had expected, God and Jesus are to be their source of strength and meaning and hope. This is the context in which further 'I am' words are given: *'I am the way, the truth, and the life; no one comes to the Father except by me.'* (John 14:6) It is in following Jesus that we shall come to our eternal destiny: when the meaning of everything becomes clouded under the pressure of events, who Jesus is and what he stands for is the one true guide; he is the source of life – even when everything seems to be conspiring to overwhelm us. Above all, these words need to be taken together because they provide the ultimate destiny for all God's children in returning to the Father, as Jesus is about to do.

Jesus expounds the unity between the Father and the Son (as the Prologue set out), and that same bond of love and obedience needs to exist between the Son and his disciples. This is a different way to approach discipleship – not in terms of outward actions but through an inner bond which binds master and disciple together. In this context, all questions have an answer; just at the moment the disciples are full of questions: *'Lord, show us the Father, we ask no more;' 'Lord, how has it come about that you mean to disclose yourself to us and not to the world?'* It is not answers expressed in words that will give any satisfaction; that only comes as the disciples learn to trust and love and obey. And as they do that, they will also receive a further gift – Christ's parting gift of peace, that deep, abiding assurance which external circumstances cannot take away.

It seems that with the command, *'come, let us go!'* (John 14:31) Jesus' words to the disciples are finished, and it is time to move towards the next stage of the drama. Yet chapter 15 begins as if nothing has happened: Jesus is still speaking; the subject is still discipleship, although his use of the vine enables him to present a different picture of the relationship between the disciple and his master. The disciple can do nothing on his own; only if he remains an integral part of the vine can he blossom and produce a rich harvest. This gives rise to another picture, *'Dwell in my love.'* So simple is the idea that it needs no explanation, but it expresses the way the disciple comes to find his life and strength in his master and Lord. Again, the command to love is spoken, but Jesus develops what he has already said, *'There is no greater love than this, that someone should lay down his life for his friends.'* (John 15:13) It is not only that Jesus is about to die to bring forgiveness and salvation to those who believe in him (and in that way give them an example), there is also a development in the closeness between master and disciple: the master calls his disciples 'friends' and the fruit of this new depth of relationship is a greater awareness of the purposes and will of God. As friends, they will be treated much as their master and Lord has been treated, but instead of his physical presence with them, they will have the Spirit to guide and strengthen and encourage them.

With the promise of the Spirit, Jesus' focus moves ahead to the parting so soon to come. They will feel bereft, but they will not be alone; indeed, if they are to grow into this greater discipleship Jesus has outlined it will be necessary for Jesus to return to the Father, so that the new relationship can develop. With the mention of Jesus going away the questions begin once more, but as the conversation draws to its close the disciples express for the first time their confidence in Jesus and all that he has taught them: *'Now you are speaking plainly, not in figures of speech! We are certain now that you know everything, and do not need to be asked; because of this we believe that you have come from God.'* (John 16:30) In the final verse of this chapter are words of victory through suffering: *'But take heart! I have conquered the world.'* Whatever may seem to be unfolding in the next few hours, the outcome is certain. The victory he will win is not just for himself, but for his disciples and all who come to follow him.

One final act of love before Jesus and his disciples leave the upper room and make their way across the Kidron valley to the garden where they have met before on so many occasions is Jesus' prayer. Chapter 17 is what has come to be known as Jesus' 'High-Priestly Prayer.' It is unlike anything we have heard before. It is not a brief, direct and focused prayer. Like the rest of the Gospel it seems to meander over many different subjects. It is both a loving communion of the Son with the Father, a commending into the Father's keeping those whom God has given him, a prayer for those who will, in the future, come to believe, and a consecration of Jesus himself to what must lie ahead. It brings to its conclusion this intimate time of sharing with the disciples the hidden truths which stand behind the events so soon to take place. It has been pretty well the only time in the Gospel when anything like instruction of the disciples has been recorded, which makes it uniquely important, and the heart of it – the bond between the disciple and his master – remains a priceless insight in any generation.

The time has now come to move beyond words and instruction to the drama through which Jesus completes the task laid on him by the Father.

The Passion Narrative

Up to this point, John's Gospel has been utterly different from the others. From the beginning of the Prologue to his account of the Last Supper, John has offered us a perspective on Christ, his life and ministry, which has rarely used the same material. On the few occasions that he records stories and events that are familiar from the other Gospels, his treatment of them is totally different. We must expect the same with the Passion Narrative and his account of the resurrection of Christ. John is not wanting to say 'they've got it wrong; this is the way things really happened.' His concern is to set out his account of the passion so that his readers will be able to understand the profound significance of the events he is presenting. It is not the differences with the other Gospels on which we should focus our attention; rather, John's theological perspective will speak to his readers, through the events of the passion, of God's ultimate purpose and commitment to be seen on the cross. Here we will see why John the Baptist called Jesus 'The Lamb of God;' here we will come to understand what kind of king he is; here we will see Jesus raised on the cross to bring salvation and healing to all who look to him. These are the themes which run deep within the story he presents. From beginning to end, this is a theological work-and it is for theology above all that we should look as we read John's Passion Narrative. We should not be surprised at the many differences, small and large, which we find between the accounts of the other Gospels and chapters 18 and 19, and especially his account of the resurrection (chapters 20 and 21). Jesus and the disciples go to a garden on leaving the upper room, but the garden is not named. There is no agony in the garden and no prayer recorded. Though clearly the disciples must have scattered, there is no mention of this. Instead, despite a very considerable arresting party (Temple police and soldiers) it is Jesus who is very much in command of the situation. He comes forward to ask who they are looking for, and when they answer, *'Jesus of Nazareth,'* and Jesus says *'I am he,'* John says, *'they drew back and fell to the ground.'* (John 18:5) It is Jesus who gives the orders: *'let these others go'*; and later to Peter, *'Put away your sword.'* There is no act of betrayal by Judas (even though he is with the arresting party). The final words of this account give the reason for this way of describing the events: *'This is the cup the Father has given me; shall I not drink it?'* (John 18:11) Jesus facilitates the arrest so that he can do the Father's will. This is the theological point; how it worked out in fact must have been very different.

The next surprise is that Jesus was taken to Annas, Caiaphas' father-in-law. Jesus, according to John's account, is not sent to Caiaphas until after he has been questioned (there is no mention of any examination before Caiaphas in John's Gospel, never mind the Sanhedrin) and the questions themselves did not elucidate any evidence that was in any way incriminating. It does, however, give the opportunity for John to relate his account of Peter's denial of Jesus.

Jesus was led to the governor's headquarters. John notes that the Jews did not go in, in order not to be defiled, so that they could eat the feast. This brings us to the question of the timing of the crucifixion. John's account is entirely different from the way events are set out in the other Gospels. That, perhaps, is no surprise: since the first chapter, John has spoken of Jesus as the Lamb of God, and in order to chime in with this identification of Jesus with the Lamb whose blood on the doorpost at Passover meant that the angel of death would 'pass over', he records Jesus' death at the moment when the Passover Lambs are killed. Despite the fact that Jesus' arrest is portrayed as being at their initiative, the Jews seem very reluctant to be precise about the charge against Jesus. At first, they simply call Jesus a criminal, and when Pilate suggests that they should try him by their own law, they reply that they are not allowed to put anyone to death. Only at the third time of asking does Pilate discover that Jesus is the King of the Jews – and now he must be involved, because that is a political charge. It seems impossible that the conversation which follows could have taken place between Jesus and Pilate. John is not trying to relay an actual conversation that happened, but he has his points to make and this seems the only way of doing it. Jesus is king – but not in an earthly sense with a physical kingdom and armies and all the usual trappings of power. So when Pilate asks him if he is a king, he replies *"King" is your word.'* He speaks to Pilate of a different kingdom (just as he spoke to the Samaritan woman about 'living' water and to the crowd in chapter 6 about food that will last). Two understandings of 'kingdom' are present in this conversation, but which is the true kingdom, the physical temporal one or the kingdom from beyond? Jesus points beyond; this is the truth he came to proclaim. Pilate, caught up in the temporal physical kingdom, retorts, *'What is truth?'* but from that moment on does all he can to release Jesus. But the crowd would have none of it: *'We want Barabbas!'* was their demand. John's only comment on this turn of events ends the chapter: *'Barabbas was a bandit.'*

Once again John departs from the order we find in the other Gospels; it makes little sense to have Jesus mocked and scourged before any sentence is passed, but we have some way to go before a final decision is made. It seems that Pilate was hoping that the sight of a humiliated and beaten Jesus might change the minds of the Jews. If so, the chorus of *'Crucify! Crucify!'* was enough to show him that the strategy did not work, and draws from him a petulant *'Take him yourselves and crucify him'* (which he knows they cannot do; crucifixion is a Roman means of execution which the Jews had no power to practise).

But worse was to come: the reason why Jesus must die is that *'he claimed to be the Son of God'* and when even that did not clinch it, the Jews played the ultimate card: *'If you let this man go you are no friend to Caesar; anyone who claims to be a king is opposing Caesar.'* We might have expected a formal pronouncement when Pilate took his seat, but John simply records that he *'handed Jesus over to be crucified.'* But John has a different reason for setting it out like this: 'handed over' is precisely the term used when a lamb is brought for sacrifice. He intends us to see that Christ, the sinless (spotless, and so suitable for the holy act of sacrifice), is handed over as the Lamb of God to take away sin and restore the right relationship between God and those for whom the lamb is offered.

The crucifixion is recorded in two short verses (John 19:17-18). There is no mention of pain or the horror of the moment. Instead, John records a quarrel about the wording of the public notice fastened to the cross, and the way the soldiers on duty at the execution haggled over Jesus' clothes. John includes a text of scripture (this is unusual for John, but at the crucifixion the scriptures are invoked three times to underline that all that is happening is according to God's great plan) which completes this episode. Around the cross are some of Jesus' closest friends and his own mother. At the moment of her desolation he commends her to the care of his closest disciple, and so fulfils his duty towards his mother. Two further words bring us to the completion of his life: *'I am thirsty,'* speaks of Jesus fulfilling all that scripture prophesied about him; *'It is accomplished'* brings him to the moment of death. It is towards this moment that the Gospel has been bringing us since the very first chapter. The task for which he came into the world has been completed. He lays down his life, in order to take it up again (John 10:18). For once death is not the end, is not defeat or the point of no return. All that is transformed, and Jesus, in being lifted up on the cross, has become the one who is able to give eternal life to those who look to him.

So much that is familiar is missing from John's account: there is no darkness, no mockery from bystanders or those who were crucified with him, no words of desolation from Psalm 22, nor does the centurion acknowledge Jesus to be Son of God. From beginning to end of the Passion Narrative, Jesus has been driving the drama forward; it is his obedience and self-giving which reaches its climax on the cross.

But John does not allow us to dwell on this moment. The time-setting John has given to the crucifixion means that things need to be done for the proper observance of the religious festivities. The bodies must be removed so that they do not defile a most important Sabbath. Breaking the legs of those being crucified would hasten the death of those on the crosses; then there was nothing to prevent them being removed before the Sabbath observance began at sunset. In Jesus' case, that was not necessary, and modern understanding of water and blood coming out of Jesus' side confirms that Jesus is already dead. But John includes this moment not for scientific confirmation of his death, but rather that water and blood were symbolic of the two sacramental moments (Baptism and the Eucharist) when those united with Christ share in his death and resurrection. The whole account is rounded off with two words from scripture: *'No bone of his shall be broken;'* and *'They shall look on him whom they pierced.'* (John 19:36-37) These confirm that all that has happened has been according to God's will set out in the scriptures many years before.

The taking down of the bodies and the hasty burial are also related by John, but once again John's account is rather different. Nicodemus joins Joseph of Arimathaea and together they remove the body. John, however, tells of spices – *'a mixture of myrrh and aloes, more than half a hundredweight'* – and strips of linen being used *'following the Jewish burial customs'* before the body is placed in the tomb. This is rather different from the picture presented by the other Gospels, but serves to underline that Jesus was dead and was properly treated as a dead body by those who took care of him. Nothing was left undone; this was the final act of devotion which followers of him could perform.

Resurrection and Endings

The final chapters of John's Gospel stand out from the rest of the Gospel in a number of ways. After a book that has expressed its message through what was said in the arguments and controversies between Jesus and the Jews, and then in the teaching Jesus gives to the disciples at the Last Supper, we are now given straight storytelling with all its power to communicate at more than one level. There are no explanations or qualifications of any kind until we come to the two endings (John 20:30-31; and 21:25) which are both clearly editorial material not belonging to the account itself. These two chapters make wonderful use of the means of communication mostly used by the other Gospels. We are in familiar territory, with a storyline which has continuity, and which builds to a conclusion, the truth and the message being found in the story itself. Such is the clarity of what we are told that no commentary or explanation is needed – indeed its absence only adds to the power of the presentation.

For generations of Christians, it is John's account of the resurrection events which speaks most powerfully of the reality and truth of Easter, and which surpasses all other attempts to express the depth and the glory of the experience of the risen Lord. In comparison, the other accounts of the resurrection somehow feel less than satisfying. John includes what we need: his account begins with the desolation most of us know at the death of a loved one, and in this way Easter begins where we are. The empty tomb produces agony, not discovery of the truth, and the anxiety of Mary Magdalene and the race of the two disciples are all part of the raw nerves these moments bring.

The encounter of Mary with the risen Lord in the garden begins with pain, not recognition, and it is only when Jesus speaks her name (as only he would speak it) that the veil of sorrow and bereavement is stripped away.

The appearance of Jesus that evening to a whole group of disciples together brings the story to another level, and the brief encounter fills out the significance of what we have been shown. But that is not all. The faithful Thomas was not there, and he would have none of the cheap 'Jesus is alive' talk the disciples regaled him with until he himself experienced the risen Lord, and he exclaimed, *'My Lord and my God!'* Jesus' response to this might well have made an ideal ending: *'Because you have seen me you have found faith. Happy are they who find faith without seeing me.'*

At some point or other verses 30 and 31 were added. These are by a different hand, and expressed the purpose of this book in ways more reminiscent of the other gospels than of the mind which spoke of the 'Word' in the Prologue. It speaks of *'this book'* but that does not necessarily mean the Gospel of John as we have it now. It is not the only time that an episode has been given a firm ending, only for the same pattern to continue in the next verse as if nothing had happened (see end of chapter 14). So too now, chapter 21 begins with the slightest of links, but tells of events in Galilee when Jesus appeared to his disciples after his resurrection. Once again, the pattern of storytelling is of a high quality, and the whole chapter builds to Jesus' words to Peter, *'Follow me'* (verses 19-22). There are, of course, nice touches (Jesus offers the fishermen, who have caught nothing, breakfast – including fish!) and Peter's restoration has all the human feeling of a man, who is aware of his own failures, being invited to make a fresh start – indeed to take on even greater responsibilities despite his past mistakes. Resurrection is about new beginnings for the disciples as well as their Lord, and this is the point that these final stories present.

The Gospel ends with what seems like a guarantee of its authenticity. Not quite, 'I was there; I have recorded these things which I personally experienced: what I say is true.' It is the record of someone who was. How we would love this Gospel to be by John 'the beloved disciple' - but although it ends on that note, the Gospel itself has a different story to tell - and it is to this that we must now turn.

What the Gospel says about itself

The Gospel of John raises particular problems, not just of the textual kind. The long-standing tradition that the Apostle John went to Ephesus with the mother of Jesus, and lived there into ripe old age is the first piece of the jigsaw. How accurate the tradition is historically is difficult to assess, but there are great men of the early second century who give some credence to this possibility. It would be remarkable to have such a witness to the life of Jesus as the author of this Gospel, and the closing chapters which speak of the resurrection in such a direct and clear way might well support such a conclusion. But those chapters stand out from the rest of the Gospel so strongly, both in style and method of communicating, that it would be impossible to affirm that the whole of the Gospel comes to us directly from the Apostle John.

It should be noted also how this Gospel stands out from the other Gospels, not only in style but in content and shape, and particularly in the material used. It seems astonishing that there are no parables such as we find in all the other Gospels; it is equally remarkable that the teaching on prayer and discipleship which play such a considerable part in Matthew and Luke have no parallels in John; indeed, what teaching John gives us about discipleship approaches the subject in an entirely different way. If Matthew drew his material from the life of the Church, and Luke in his researches gathered his many unique contributions from people who had been eye-witnesses (or very close to them), the origins of much of John's material must be from elsewhere, and have a different history. There is almost a cultural difference, the first three Gospels springing from the life of the faith community which was in every way very close to the Jewish roots from which the faith sprang, while John expresses his deepest convictions in terms of *logos*, and through the 'I am' sayings.

One other feature of John's Gospel must be taken into account. Our expectation of a Gospel is that it tells a story – that there is continuity, with a beginning and an end, and points along the way at which we can see how the drama develops. But this is not what John's Gospel presents us with. Individual events and the subsequent discussions and disagreements are placed side by side with hardly any link or sense of continuity. Jesus is first in Galilee, then in Jerusalem, and then once more in Galilee; there are even two moments in the Gospel when an episode seems to have been brought to an end, only for the same or very similar subjects to be taken up, as if no closure at all had been attempted (the endings of chapter 14 and 20 spring to mind). It is as if someone has selected a number of subjects which should be presented, and has simply taken the relevant files off the shelf and placed them together without any chronological link between them (and so without any natural development of the bigger picture).

If we also take into account John's unique style of presenting the differences between Jesus and his adversaries – not to mention the similar style which characterises the conversations at the last supper – it would seem that there are several different ingredients to the make-up of this Gospel. The content suggests that it came into its present shape at a time of considerable controversy and conflict between the Christian community and those representing the Jewish faith – there seems no other explanation for the way controversy and opposition set the tone for so much of the first half of the Gospel. It may well be that the prevailing culture around the Christian community from which this Gospel sprang was largely Greek, though not necessarily in Greece itself. Certainly, the absence of parable and wisdom material, and the use of the 'I am' sayings support this, and suggest a background where ideas and concepts are more widely used than images and pictures. Supremely, the use of *logos* in the all important opening verses suggests a world where Greek philosophy is understood and undergirds the accepted way of thinking.

The variety of material in the Gospel also suggests that there were several different sources from which material came, each with its own history: there is some material which is close to its apostolic source; some is also the product of long and deep reflection; there are also other passages forged and put together under the pressure of religious conflict, and showing deep scars from powerful disagreement. All these different kinds of material, however, also bear the signs of an oral origin. There are almost no lists in John; time and again we find the author going back on something or even correcting what he has already said. Rarely do we find a logical working out of the themes under discussion as a writer would naturally do; there is too much cut and thrust, changing tack, thinking on the spur of the moment.

How, then, do we account for this astonishing, unpredictable, profound and glorious Gospel? Perhaps we shall never be able to. I would suggest, however, that something like the following would account for much of this:

> Some of the material, the resurrection stories especially, demand some direct apostolic link, albeit removed by at least a generation, but revered and preserved over a period of time. At some point, a very considerable mind has drawn together the Prologue and its witness to Christ which is expressed so succinctly. Other material too, not least the combative chapters, was created in the heat of battle but remembered and treasured, not least because the person who first framed it was also revered and remembered within the community. Last, but not least, there needs to have been an editor whose choice of material and wide knowledge of the varied traditions in the community has given us the Gospel in its present shape.

The virtue of such a very general outline is that there is always room to discover or understand more! It also serves as a picture – no more – of the origins of the material of which the Gospel is made up. Most importantly, the outline given suggests that it took time, considerable time, for the Gospel we know as the Gospel according to Saint John to come into being, and that there are contributions from a number of people over a period. The result is sometimes difficult, often challenging, but in John's Gospel we have a treasure which stands for all time and speaks to every generation. As such it is priceless, and we are immensely the richer for being able to read and study it.

CHAPTER SIX

What the Gospels Teach us

If it comes as a surprise that the Gospels are such very different works, brought into existence for such diverse reasons, can they remain for us the sacred, holy and irreplaceable books they have been for nearly two thousand years? Nothing that has been written in this study takes away from their value and importance; if anything, this study has been undertaken so that anyone who turns to the Gospels can be helped to understand better what we have inherited from the very early days of the Christian faith. The purpose has been to take seriously what we have received, to listen to what the Gospels have said about themselves, so that we have a context which brings focus to our study and use of each book. They remain the main source of our knowledge of Jesus – and for those who believe and seek to follow him there can hardly be anything more important – the foundation documents which furnish us with all we need in order to live the Christian life. This was their role when they were first brought together in the second century; that remains their role now for every believer or enquirer.

The unique importance of the Gospels remains. They speak of Christ, and he shows us the will and compassion and purpose of the Father in word and deed. These are still things to ponder and learn from with care and reflection, meditating on all that we are given, and coming close to God as we hear the words of Christ or watch him with our mind's eye moving among people and touching their lives in so many different ways. Christians of every generation have done this. It is hoped that this study enables its readers to be more confident in opening the Gospels – above all that the apparent differences between the Gospels are less puzzling.

What we have discovered, however, must be taken further. If the different approaches of the Gospels have shown us anything, it is that the experience of Jesus, his teaching, indeed the whole impact of his life, death and resurrection speak to us in many different ways. We must be at least as flexible as the Gospel-writers; it is, after all, their freedom to use the material they had at their disposal which has given us the Gospels we have. Two further clues they give us: not only does each Gospel suggest by its make-up and content how it was first used; by using each for the same purpose, we may well find that we get most out of them. It may also be that by learning how the early Church went about bringing its core documents into being, we, two thousand years later, can learn from them how best to go about our business of sharing the good news of Jesus with our contemporaries, how we set out patterns of discipleship, and commend the faith of Jesus in a sceptical and sometimes hostile world. With this in mind we can now revisit each Gospel, and see the help we might be given in the world of today.

The Word Person to Person

It is not always easy to make the adjustment when we are invited to see something from a different standpoint. The mind has a habit of slipping back into old patterns of thinking, especially patterns some of us have used for many years. It goes against the grain to think of the Gospel according to St Mark as an oral work, when everything we have known hitherto has invited us to think of it and use it as a written document. Yet the evidence is there: it has no literary form, such as we find in the other Gospels; it uses all the strengths of the oral, almost none of the written word. The storyline is strong, with the momentum being sustained sometimes by little devices which both link events and give a sense of immediacy which drives the work forward. The brevity of the language is unmatched elsewhere, and the storyline invites us to be engaged with it as events unfold. Everything is included within the storyline; editorial comment is almost entirely absent, and nowhere does the storyteller step out of character to explain or inform; lists are mostly missing, and there are none of the smooth literary touches which might tidy up the account – especially the end of the Gospel. The ending is sudden, raw and leaves its audience almost in a state of shock; no one would plan such an end for a book – but when it is spoken we are left sharing the shock of resurrection breaking into our world, where death is so universally expected to be the end. What looks so negative, so like a defeat, so unsatisfactory – *They said nothing to anyone because they were overcome with fear*' (Mark 16:8) – speaks of an experience which has ever since been at the very heart of the Christian faith.

In a world which looks for facts and explanations, Mark speaks with a different voice. He shares with us the impact of the person of Jesus – what those who heard or saw Jesus experienced as he ministered to people in their need and spoke to them of the kingdom of God. The authors (those who by their sharing of the gospel shaped the way the 'Jesus story' was told) of this Gospel would have been very disappointed in us if all we had gleaned from their words was a certain amount of information about the historical Jesus. Their purpose was not only to inform, but to transform – to change hearts and minds by helping their audience to share and respond to the experience and impact of Jesus. It is not that Jesus was not historical: the authors of this Gospel, along with the other Gospel-writers, saw no need to prove the existence of a man they had seen and heard and touched and known. This is wholly taken for granted because, after all they had experienced, there seemed absolutely no need to waste time on such utterly basic matters. In the case of this Gospel, many of those who first heard it may well already have been aware of the person of Jesus; some may even have met him.

The authors use life's great educator – experience – to achieve their purpose. It is, of course, the perfect medium. In all kinds of ways – and from our earliest moments – experience has been the way we have learned and understood, and got a feel for whatever confronts us. We learn not only about the world and ourselves; experience enables us to make our own assessment of events and encounters, people and actions. While analysis allows us to stand back, to examine and consider (somewhat as a spectator looking on), experience helps us to understand and evaluate from within. 'Getting the feel' for an occasion gives us more than facts and an accurate description: it enables us to make a response not of the mind alone, but of the will and the heart. How often it is experience which changes minds when arguments have proved fruitless; it is experience which speaks to the whole person, and engages the whole person in the response that is made.

St Mark's Gospel springs from experience, and speaks in such a way that the audience is able to share not only a spectator's view of Jesus' ministry, but also what many of the events felt like and meant to those who were present. Thus, as was pointed out in chapter 2, the responses of the people on so many occasions in the early chapters of the Gospel not only described what was happening, but pointed the listeners to the inner significance of it as well. Christ is presented so that those who hear the Gospel are given the opportunity to encounter the person of Christ, and respond to the impact of his presence and his actions. Faith is the goal, and the Gospel is so constructed that those who listen with more than half an ear will be given all they need to respond with faith and in action.

There is one unique side of experience which is often overlooked. No one can take it away; it becomes part of the person caught up in it – not least because it changes that individual – and even when years pass and memory fades, it remains part of the developing story of each life involved. Not all experience comes with a clear meaning attached. Often things puzzle;

sometimes an experience leaves us utterly baffled, and only later does the penny drop and some kind of meaning dawns. The experience which has framed St Mark's Gospel comes with meaning attached, so that we, the listeners (or readers), do not need to tease out the secret of the story being shared with us. It is laid out for us to grasp or reject.

The sharing of experience is most naturally done by word of mouth, person to person. It is never an objective activity, putting distance between the speaker and his subject. Those who first began telling the Good News of Jesus may well have spoken in personal terms to begin with, but what had begun with 'I saw' or 'We heard him say,' soon dropped the personal pronoun while still relating the fundamental experience. Such 'Gospel-telling' retains all the power and directness of experience, even though the speaker is further removed from the raw experience. Development of this process will have been inevitable, yet its nature remains. Content will have been expanded and refined by the need to include particular material which would help those who are being caught up in the sharing of the experience of Jesus to make a fuller response. The telling of the Good News achieved one other thing: it managed to bridge the gap between the listeners and Christ. This is, after all, the nature of news. It bridges gaps of distance and time. St Mark's Gospel achieves this: it is the best possible kind of news.

Those coming to this Gospel today, whether they hear it or read it, are still being caught up in the experience which prompted the first Christians to tell others about Jesus. Above all, this Gospel will help them to 'get the feel' of the events as they unfold, and Jesus becomes more of a living person rather than an historical figure. Its task is still to bring to faith – but for many of us it is also to renew the faith that has often become overgrown with questions and complications in the course of life. The central call is still 'Renounce self; take up your cross and follow me.' But for this call to discipleship to take root, every person to whom the call comes must be enabled to look beyond self and its many insistent demands. Only two things make that possible: love and faith – faith in particular which is not so much a rational assent to particular propositions, as a response of admiration, trust, loyalty and commitment to One who is true and unfailing and strong. So love and faith become the driving forces in life, and these create lives of both stature and action.

For the Christian community, this Gospel gives us the tongue to speak of Jesus in a way we often find difficult. Perhaps it is one of the consequences of having Gospels written down that we have become book-bound in our approach to communicating our message, and tongue-tied in our efforts to share it with others. It may be one of the subliminal messages of St Mark's

Gospel that we must be more ready to trust our experience, and in that we should include both our own personal experience, and the experiences that are shared with us through the words of the Gospel. They are the means by which we give voice to why we believe, what faith means to us, and the change it makes when we look beyond ourselves to the One we call our Lord and Saviour. It is a bit unfair, perhaps, to refer to Paul Tillich's 'the ground of our being,' or the more widely used 'the man for others,' titles given to our Lord some fifty years ago, but both are examples of the way this bookish trend has tended to put distance between ourselves and our Lord, and we have come to express the faith increasingly in philosophical and impersonal ways. There is a place for that, but it is not the way in which we come to faith, let alone have our lives lit up and changed by what faith gives us. The Gospel of Mark remains personal and direct. Above all, 'follow me' calls for both close attention to Christ and a love and loyalty towards him which rises above all other calls and commitments.

St Mark's Gospel, like the others, can be used in many different ways, but the nature and content of this Gospel suggests that its primary use should be, as it was in the very beginning, to bring to faith, and to refresh faith which over the years may have become over-complicated. The pressure to make the case to a sceptical world has all too often meant that Christians have been concerned to give reasons and explanations. That is not Mark's first priority. Listen to him; share the impact of Jesus' presence, power and teaching, and respond to it with heart and will. That is the use to which this Gospel is best suited.

Holy Book: a Different Kind of Reading

Matthew comes to us with the label of a Gospel, but its nature and content suggest that we must use it in a very different way from the other books ranked alongside it. From beginning to end Matthew was writing scripture, in his mind at least a kind of writing set apart from any other. Its singular purpose was to provide for the Christian Church what the Old Testament gave to the Jewish people – its credentials as the Chosen People: the Jewish scriptures gave them a history from which they could trace their origins, have a common identity, and an understanding of who they were; their unique relationship with God was set out in detail in the Covenant, and through laws and commandments their side of the Covenant was recorded so that all could follow it. All this and much more provided an authoritative core for their life as a people, and enabled them to know who they were, despite exile and conquest and the national crises which came upon them. Matthew set out to provide all this for the young Christian community. He gave it a story –

largely the story of Jesus, but it also included the disciples and the authority he invested in them. There was a new set of commandments in the Beatitudes, and copious instructions on how to follow the Christian way. He even gives them Jesus' final instructions, so that they could be confident of the task laid upon them by their risen and ascended Lord. Perhaps more important still is his understanding that in writing the Christian scripture he was not only following the pattern set out for him in the Old Testament: what he wrote completed, by design, the story begun in the earlier books of scripture.

All this Matthew has achieved in a masterly fashion, and the book which has come to us as the Gospel according to St Matthew adds enormously to the knowledge and understanding of the Christian community about who they are and what are their true credentials. The role of core texts, as Matthew's Gospel is, is a common phenomenon in almost every religion – but surprisingly not only in religion. The writings of Marx were utterly central to the working out and practice of communism. More recently *The Origin of Species* by Charles Darwin has almost been accorded the respect usually reserved for holy writ – and its devotees have gone a great deal further than Darwin in the importance and credence they have given to it. It seems that even secular philosophies, never mind religions, have the need for core documents which express the convictions they adhere to. It is a universal pattern, but perhaps it can be seen more clearly in the secular world where there is no halo that can be placed around what is written on religious grounds. Commonly, both credence and respect are shown to such core documents; it is a value invested in them, not something demanded by the document itself. This means that it is treated and used in certain ways, which go far beyond the nature of the document: the reader approaches the text with expectation, seeking to learn and discover – but also to take what they have discovered and work it out in other areas of life, not just in philosophy or the sciences. How very like religion, which is so often specifically rejected!

This brief glance away from Matthew's Gospel nevertheless illustrates the manner in which the author hoped and expected his Gospel to be used. The reader is expected to come to the text with the same respect and credence that people bring to core documents; each is to receive and learn, rather than engage in the rough and tumble of ordinary reading. In what is being laid out there is no expectation of critical examination, but through reflection it is intended to enrich understanding and shape the pattern of discipleship in the reader or the community. Matthew invites us to a very different kind of reading; the centrepiece of the book is crafted precisely so that this reflective style of reading will result in well-ordered discipleship. From the Beatitudes, through Christ's very different commands – *They were told . . . but what I tell you is this . . .'* (Matthew 5) – to teaching about fasting and prayer Matthew leads us to the final parable which demands action, not just a nodding acquaintance with what is written. There is almost an assumption that whoever picks up this book and reads it is part of the faith community; there is no thought that the Christian way will be lived in any other circumstances.

Matthew, then, not only sets out to write scripture; he invites his readers to treat his Gospel as scripture should be treated. Not only does he have a specific role for his writing; he gives his readers a specific role as well – as learners, disciples, followers who must come to *'understand'* (Matthew 13:51). This is not a role the modern mind readily adopts. Today, we come with questions, almost demanding that what we read shall give us answers – and answers in the terms we have set out by our questions. We shall be disappointed in our reading of Matthew if we ignore the role he has given us. While his Gospel contains information in plenty and copious directions on living the life of a disciple, 'understanding' is above all what he wants for us, and 'understanding' comes mostly through meditation and reflection. For all scripture speaks human language, yet the real message is of God, his will, his way and his command.

This Gospel expects to speak above all to the Christian community. It addresses the Church, and tells it what it stands for. It gives it an identity, so that it can be confident enough about itself not to turn inward with doubt and questioning, but be clear about the task laid upon it by its Lord and King. But if it speaks to the Church community first, it also has much to say to every individual believer. They are to be 'Blessed' – 'Salt of the Earth' – 'Light for the World,' so that although the discipline of Christ's way is inward and spiritual, each is called to be engaged in the world, to reconcile and transform, teach and serve those among whom they are set. It is more than good news: it provides for the Christian community its credentials and its marching orders.

Apology and Persuasion

St Luke provides an almost complete contrast to Matthew. He is writing for those who are outside the faith community. He expects his readers to know very little of the story he is to tell, and because hearsay and rumour have already done their work, he is conscious that what he says must change minds and persuade, if the Christian way is to be accepted, even if it is not actively followed. Somehow he must demonstrate that Christ and those who follow him are neither subversive nor wicked nor dangerous. They do, already, have a reputation. Christians had often been the focus of disturbances and unrest – and worse. The Jews especially were loud in their animosity towards them.

The Empire had already decided that the Jews needed special treatment; was this offshoot of the Jewish faith going to be just as troublesome?

Luke sets about his task with consummate care. The opening verses both of his Gospel and the Acts of the Apostles underline just how careful he is to use whatever tools he can to inform and persuade. He is making a serious case for the truth and blamelessness both of Jesus and his followers, so his opening words follow the conventions of the world of his day. Anyone reading them would understand that a substantial case is about to be laid out; from the opening they would know what to expect. Although Jesus is a Jewish figure, sent by God to fulfil God's promises to the Jewish people, Luke has placed him firmly in the Roman world, and in this way affirms that Jesus has a place in this world, however Jewish he might be. In the pages of this Gospel, Luke follows a convention well known in the wider world: he presents Jesus, his origins, his deeds, his teaching in the way many other lives have been recorded. If this Gospel looks more like a biography than any other, that is no surprise. But this is no biography, despite its birth to death (and beyond) storyline. There is purpose far beyond the details of his account: he is commending to his readers Jesus the teacher, the healer, the man of prayer, the man of compassion and understanding, who neither courts power nor commends it to his followers. From his humble beginnings (no threat to the Empire there, then) to his death, demanded by his own people despite both Pilate and Herod finding nothing worthy of death, the Jesus presented by Luke is none of the things his detractors loudly assert. This 'troublemaker' was always the victim of the anger and rejection of others – and we see in the Acts of the Apostles just how true this is for his followers as well; he was not the instigator of violent revolution – and if Luke wrote after AD 70 the rebellion of the Jews and the sacking of Jerusalem would have been wildly known. Whoever Jesus was, he stood out from the actions and ways of his fellow-countrymen, and so did his followers.

But Luke's message to his readers went a great deal further than simply addressing the way the Christian faith was viewed in wider society. However important that was, Luke was not going to waste the opportunity. He had got the ear of his readers; he was determined to make the most of the opportunity. In setting out the case for the Christian faith not to be viewed with suspicion, he offers a great deal more. In the story of Christ's birth we have not only the human story; the songs of Zachariah and Mary praise God for the revolution he was bringing about – freedom to worship and live in faith; the humble lifted high – the human story rings with the message of a God who fulfils his promises and treats with dignity and tenderness those who carry life's burdens.

When it comes to teaching (chapter 6) he addresses the injustices of life; his two great themes are 'love your enemies' and 'do not judge.' As the Gospel unfolds, the healing, feeding and teaching speak through Christ of a God of compassion and wholeness; all are embraced: a centurion has his servant healed; a Samaritan is given the leading role in one of Jesus' stunning parables. The Christ of this Gospel has broken out of the limitations that had come to confine the Jewish heritage; Christ included, where the Jewish way excluded. Christ spoke of God's forgiveness; they invoked the law (chapter 15).

In his account of Jesus' death, Luke is at great pains not only to establish the innocence of Jesus; we see how, even in the middle of suffering and rejection, he is open to the anguish of the women of Jerusalem, he prays for the soldiers, even as they inflict excruciating pain, and responds with understanding and hope to the words of the penitent thief. No one reading this can be in any doubt that a whole new way of living is being set out. But perhaps it is in his account of the resurrection that we can see how Luke sets about communicating the Christian message. He is no longer trying simply to justify the Christian faith and those who follow it, but with great care he writes to make it possible for his readers to be led to faith as the Christian story unfolds. He is aware that he is writing for a sceptical audience; talk of resurrection would easily be scoffed at; it was usually the preserve of cranks and weird sects – not at all the kind of people to be taken seriously.

Luke's account begins where everyone else's begins – with the expectation that death means death, and the women come to the tomb to complete the burial rites. The shock of the empty tomb and the vision of angels is first related and then almost dismissed by the disciples (Luke calls them apostles), allowing the readers to hear the first evidence of the resurrection while still hanging on to their scepticism. The storyline moves on to the road to Emmaus and the astonishing experience of the two sad followers of Jesus. Luke tells this episode in such a way that the listener is drawn into both the sadness and the teaching given by the stranger, making the death of Christ and his resurrection so much more credible. Finally, the audience is brought to the moment of recognition in the familiar action of the breaking of bread. Luke makes sure that his readers are able to share the whole process of coming to faith as the two followers put their experience into words. All that they have come to believe is then confirmed when they make their way back to Jerusalem, and share their news with the apostles. The final proof is given with the appearance of Jesus, and his demonstration that he is truly alive by eating some fish which they give him: *'No ghost has flesh and blood as you can see that I have'* (Luke 24:39). Luke enables his readers to make a journey of discovery and faith much as Jesus' first followers had.

With this in mind, it is a little easier to see with what care Luke has made the case for the Christian faith to his readers, and how he has shaped what he has written to ignite the spark of faith. This Gospel is a judicious mixture of fact, experience and response. He has been highly selective in his choice of material. He includes little touches we find nowhere else – the trip to Jerusalem when Jesus was twelve, and the note of his age when he began his public ministry. But he is more than willing to omit events which have played a prominent role in the account of the other Gospels. So he omits the story of Jesus walking on the water, and the other episodes which seem to repeat stories already told (including a second feeding of a great number). There are many stories of healing and restoration, but he does not tell the story of the gradual healing of a blind man. His 'sermon' is a great deal shorter, and his Beatitudes are fewer and followed by a matching set of 'woes.' His presentation of the Beatitudes is not the giving of a new set of Commandments; rather, he shows them as an expression of the will of a just and compassionate God. All the elements with strong Jewish roots are banished, and the teaching on prayer moved to a different place and setting. Even the Lord's Prayer is paired down so as not to include the clauses which are particularly of Jewish origin.

Material he does include, especially among the parables, gives a breadth and a generosity to the faith which is being presented: the parables of the prodigal son, the good Samaritan, the rich man and the poor man at his gate, the lost sheep, to mention only a very few, give the feel of welcome, restoration, of people having a way of hope and wholeness being offered to them. In this way Luke is speaking to the Roman world. While Christ fulfils all the Jewish hopes, the manner in which Luke presents him also speaks to the world beyond. He has not only set out to change minds, he has framed his presentation to enable the person and teaching of Christ to attract the attention of his readers at another level too. In the first place, it was a literate and well-educated audience who would not only appreciate the care with which he had presented the case for the Christian way, but also would themselves have been alerted to the qualities and values this way espoused.

Luke's careful and confident presentation of Christ is a model of how the Christian Gospel should be presented in a hostile and sceptical world. The world needs to hear it, because the world stands in need of the healing and restoration which is at the heart of the Gospel. It is a Gospel grounded in fact and experience; it has a vision of God which is generous and welcoming. Above all, it is not a God who is limited in his love only to the Jews and the Jewish way. Luke breaks new ground in addressing the scepticism of the world while still touching hearts as well as changing minds. It is a model for Christians in every generation. In a sceptical and secular world it is an essential guide and inspiration to a Church which has to find a way of speaking to the world around it. We would be wise to use it in this way.

The Unchanging in a Changing World

While the first three Gospels have spoken to us of Christ, and have invited us to respond to him in faith, to follow him in the way of discipleship and commend him to others for his love and compassion and divine humanity, John has brought us to Christ from a different direction. The framework of his thinking has constantly looked beyond the material and the tangible, and calls us to look through signs to the abiding truth about Jesus. What he shows us is timeless, and speaks of the relationship between the Father and the Son, and through the great *'I am'* sayings unfolds what Christ is to every believer - *'The Way, the Truth, the Life . . . the Vine, the Bread of Life, the Good Shepherd' and 'the Resurrection'*. That is, perhaps, to put it too narrowly. These descriptions of Jesus are true for all people in every age – timeless and eternal – undimmed by the changing nature of our world and our mortal lives.

John's Gospel invites us to step outside the framework of time and place so that we can be presented with the truth of Christ, not just on the human scale but in terms of the eternal God. This inevitably puts a strain on our human means of communication which are designed for this mortal, material, everyday world. So John's use of signs and the 'I am' sayings of Jesus are his way of overcoming the limitations of language in order to communicate the truth in Christ as he wants to express it. John's supreme skill was to use language which communicated in a way to which others would be able to respond. So the use of *logos* in the Prologue embraced both Greek and Jew; in the same way the 'I am' sayings not only communicated to the Jewish community that in Jesus is to be found the One who was *'in God's presence, and what God was, the Word was'* (John 1:1), but also the language picked up concepts familiar through the philosophy of Plato in the Greek world, and spoke to the Jews in the kind of terms they would have well understood. That he was able to speak to them about ultimate things while using material and familiar language is the triumph which allows us still to look beyond the framework of our world to the eternal which is the goal of all faith and all believing.

John uses our language to speak of God, who is greater than and beyond the things for which our language was designed. But anyone who speaks of God must be able to do this. What John manages to do is to frame his truths in terms that are not abstract and impersonal, and so makes it possible for every enquirer and every believer to reach out to this God who is both beyond our world and closely involved with it. But the exciting achievement of this Gospel is to do more than simply present the Christian understandings of God and the eternal in the marketplace of ideas and philosophies, faiths and religions. What he does is to say to each and every one that the fulfilment of their faith, and the glimpse of truth that they have discovered, is completed in Christ. He is the One to whom their insights and discoveries are ultimately leading them. The Christian faith is not primarily a denial of the things they value; it is an invitation to move beyond the position which each holds to a way of life that fulfils and completes what they already glimpse. In the marketplace of truths and ideas, Christ is *'the Way, the Truth and the Life.'*

Not everyone will take up the invitation which John offers; that is the freedom the Gospel gives us. But there is a cost in rejecting the offer that is made, which is writ large in the conflict chapters (3 to 10) in this Gospel. The opposition to Jesus becomes increasingly shrill and violent, spelling out the nature of the wilful rejection of that which is true. The issues at stake are not merely matters of opinion – take it or leave it, as you wish: truth has a nature, as does falsehood; faith brings with it change and transformation; disbelief hardens and stultifies. John presents Christ so that those who come to faith may live with fullness and a freedom that is not offered elsewhere.

Those who choose discipleship, however, are offered more than might be expected. So often, people make their choice, and it gives them a foundation, a fundamental rationale for life, and a position from which life can be understood and lived – this is as true for the atheist and the agnostic as it is for those who have a faith. Discipleship calls us into a living relationship; we are to be rooted and grounded in Christ, as the image of the vine in chapter 15 illustrates; we are called to love, but this is only possible because he first loved us.

The Gospel of John engages with the world of his day. Christians are called to the same kind of engagement in the modern world. The new rationalism frequently sounds highly critical of faith, but at its best it is still an attempt to find the great truths of life and to express them as clearly as possible. John gives those who believe in Christ a model with which to meet the challenge which is being presented. As we see Jesus at work, John recalls him speaking truths and bringing to the conversations ideas and understandings which are 'from beyond.' Christians must be prepared to do the same, since their experience of the life of faith gives them a further dimension which cannot be discovered by reason and logic alone. The purpose of the debate is to bring all, 'believing and unbelieving', to the greater truth which is most fully expressed in Christ. In this way, Christians are given both the mental framework and the necessary equipment to engage with the world as it feels towards a deeper understanding of the mysteries of life, and also to bring to the conversation a language and insights which offer a way through our earthbound patterns of thinking to discoveries which do not have that limitation. But while the world talks in terms of the abstract – ideas, principles, and concepts – John talks in personal terms. The Word is forever made flesh in the person of Jesus; God is eternally the Father. The Spirit is holy, the outpouring of the self-giving eternal God.

Conclusion

We gain so much in our use and understanding of the Gospels when we are prepared to see each Gospel as the work it is. We not only get closer to the heart of each Gospel, we come closer to Christ and the experiences which brought the first disciples to faith. What we have discovered by approaching the Gospels in this way is that the gap in time between the life of Christ and the records we have has been shrunk by a generation, and we are given the answer as to how it is that Gospels came into being at all. The Gospels themselves become more exciting, not less, and more accessible to the enquirer or believer, rather than being the preserve of the specialist and the scholar. The intention has been to let the Gospels live; the true test of this can only be the way people who have read this book take up the Gospels and find their faith deepened – and only you, the reader, will know that!